A SIMPLE
EXPLANATION OF
DARK PSYCHOLOGY

Dr. Reinhald Fearow

Contents

Chapter One

Dark Psychology, What Is It?

Introduction

Dark Psychology is the study of a condition in people that drives them to prey on others, which is generally suppressed. As long as people display restraint and don't act on their irrational or predatory impulses, they have the condition. A psychopath is a person who is able to act on these urges. They act erratically and without remorse when they damage or even murder other people. Their actions are erratic, uninspired, and uncontrolled. Because of this, it is critical to have an understanding of how and why this illness occurs in people and what may be done to lessen one's chances of being a victim. Dark psychology's principles will be discussed in this chapter, including the reasons why certain people act on their restrained state, and how it eventually becomes unrepressed. The following themes will be addressed:

"The Road" by Cormac McCarthy tells the narrative of a post-Apocalyptic world devastated by an unidentified tragedy that wiped off much of the planet's food supply. Survival instincts are activated when faced with a life-or-death situation. One of them is the practice of consuming the flesh of another human being as sustenance. The human race is able to keep this state under control under normal circumstances. As a result, it is not unheard of for people to demonstrate predatory impulses against other humans.

Research in dark psychology focuses on the beliefs that contribute to this kind of behavior. When someone engages in antisocial behavior, it's usually because they have a specific purpose in mind. Occasionally, however, these behaviors are shown by people who have no particular agenda. Those who study dark psychology are interested in situations like this, in which people are unwittingly prompted to behave in a certain way. People who specialize in dark psychology believe that there is a part of the human mind capable of making someone commit atrocities without intending to. One of the most common causes of psychopathy is the presence of this element in everyone, according to specialists. It is possible to speed up one's descent into this condition and commit horrendous crimes as a result of certain variables.

Many dark psychology specialists believe that everyone has a darker side to their personality. According to Leeds Beckett University psychology professor Steve Taylor, there has always been some degree of lunacy in the human race. Under some circumstances, humans will prey on others, and history has shown this. Group warfare and social unrest have been the norm throughout human history, both before and after civilization. As long as wealth and power have gone to a few, wars have been waged against the weak and downtrodden groups, and ethnic cleansing has taken place on a regular basis. These are some of the events that may be used to describe humans as savages from the viewpoint of an extraterrestrial observer.

All of these atrocities may be explained by the evil side of every human being, which lies dormant most of the time but can be reawakened under certain conditions. Most of these heinous acts took place on a large scale and were premeditated. For example, in ancient times, armies battled to conquer or expel others. Genocides have occurred simply because one side believed the other had an edge over them. Dictators have been overthrown by coup d'etat. Bloodshed, death, torture and other terrible crimes have occurred in all of these incidents. However, these occurrences have a sensible and delicate reasoning behind them. Such behaviors are carried out without any purpose in mind in dark psychology.

It's in everyone's nature to want to do damage to others for no apparent reason. Isolated incidents of someone intentionally harming, maiming or killing others will be reported in the media. Because it's so difficult to describe or explain, dark psychology has been used to study this kind of behavior in depth. Experts in this subject believe it has its roots in predatory behavior that evolved through time.

Before he discovered how to build tools and begin farming, early man lived as a predator. Predation continued unabated even after that. Humans are prone to prey since they all have the same ancestry. There is a great deal of restraint in us, and we do not go on killing sprees because we are not impulsive. We can't stop thinking about these things, yet we usually opt not to do anything about them. Most individuals have felt the want to harm others at some time in their life. As an example, a sad guy may fantasize about injuring their ex-girlfriend. Those who have been robbed at gunpoint may nevertheless be tempted to track down the criminals and beat them to smithereens. Introspection will reveal that you have considered hurting another human being. There's a rottenness residing deep inside each of us. Because it's in our nature to do things like this, it's perfectly OK. Psychopathic individuals, on the other hand, are more likely to act on their wicked ideas than a normal person would be. This restriction is what differentiates us from the rest of the animal kingdom. predators.

Chapter Two

According According to the Adlerian hypothesis, at least **99** percent of the time, human behavior may be interpreted as having a purpose. The one percent lives in a region that is referred to as the black singularity. The predatory inclinations of man are manifested here, yet the activities that are committed inside this domain serve no useful purpose. Within the confines of this domain, one's every passing idea is given physical form and given a response. If a person's intellect regresses to this singularity and they get the notion that they should burn their neighbor's home on fire, they will unquestionably act on that thought without giving it a second thought. There is no regret or sympathy in any of the acts that have been taken. When seen through the lens of a psychopath, everybody and everyone has the potential to become a victim. They believe that the victimization they dish out is warranted, thus there are no limits to how much they victimize others. A dark element is responsible for bringing about the fall of any individual into the dark singularity.

A desire to prey on or harm other people is an example of a dark element. A person who commits many murders in a row will be motivated by the desire to kill other people, just as someone who sets fires will have an overwhelming impulse to do so. Numerous convicted psychopaths have been questioned by forensic investigators, legal authorities, and researchers in an effort to comprehend how they got started on their destructive paths. In many instances, the psychopaths would have a significant dark element that rapidly propelled them into the dark singularity. After committing several acts of arson, a person who possessed the dark aspect of setting homes on fire would have been forced into the unavoidable darkness of a singularity. The psychopath would continue to feel some pressure from the dark component, which would prompt him to victimize other people by setting fire to their homes. These crimes of arson will be committed for no reason at all, not even vengeance, not even the desire for power and not even for money. The psychopath will act on whatever he or she considers to be an awful thinking without any attempt to rationalize their actions. The cravings that come from the dark aspect may be relatively readily repressed in normal persons. If it is not managed, the dark factor will lead an individual down a psychological rabbit hole known as a dark continuum.

One arrives at the black singularity by traveling along the dark continuum, which is the road that leads there. Psychologists describe the continuum as an ascending scale reflecting the level of irrationality and malice shown in one's ideas and behaviors. Because every person has a shadow aspect, they may be placed wherever along this continuum. On the other hand, the regular dark thoughts will rate rather low, and this will indicate that they are too far back on the route to going into the dark singularity and becoming psychopaths. Those who have been responsible for heinous killings will be placed farther down the black continuum. There will be less activity in the parts of their brain that are responsible for empathy and connecting with other people. After each horrendous murder, these factors will have less of an impact on a person's decision-making until they reach a point beyond which there is no turning back. At this moment, they will have crossed over into the black singularity and will no longer be plagued by any sort of remorse or conscience.

Chapter Three

It is possible to form the assumption that people are generally good-natured, considerate, and sympathetic. Many people would strongly dispute the notion that they have ever harbored sinister ideas in the depths of their brains. The reality of the matter is, however, that a portion of the human mind is essentially shadowy, and once that portion is given the opportunity to show itself, it does. It is common practice for people to ignore or downplay the shadowy aspects of their nature. Despite this, it is still possible to see it. If you have ever had the opportunity to play open world games like Grand Theft Auto (GTA), then you will have an understanding of the buried guilty pleasure that comes from the darker side of human nature. These kind of games serve as platforms that enable users to engage in harmful behavior without fear of any consequences in their actual lives. A player will insensitively and impulsively strike a helicopter with a rocket-propelled grenade, which will result in the death of everyone within the chopper. In a way similar to that described above, other characters will also be subjected to attacks from automatic guns, primitive weapons, punches, and kicks. When playing these types of games, normal people often experience dark and violent ideas that are comparable in nature to those that a psychopath might have in the real world but on a much smaller scale. People are essentially given the opportunity to indulge their latent psychopathic inclinations via the medium of video console gaming.

Because of evolution, every human being has the capacity for these dreary thoughts. The theory of evolution held that only the most adaptable species would be able to survive and pass their genes on to future generations. As a result, predation was necessary since it guaranteed the maintenance of life, the preservation of territory, and it also provided the appropriate circumstances for reproduction. Unfortunately, the fact that man finally evolved to become the most cruel creature also means that he is the most advanced example of that trait. It was necessary to use brutal force in order to battle, hunt, and kill. A pride of lions will be on the search for a buffalo to bring back for lunch today. A herd of buffaloes will work together to attack a lone lion or a family of young lion cubs with the goal of lowering the number of lions and other large predators. The vast majority of animals will exhibit comparable cruel and violent behaviors since some of these traits have protected them from extinction over the course of evolution.

As a result, aggression and bloodthirstiness are already ingrained in the majority of animals. However, man is the only animal that hunts for reasons other than ensuring its own survival and offspring's offspring's survival. In the case of birds, for example, it is unheard of for one bird to go about and demolish the nests that other birds have made for no apparent reason. In addition, there have been no accounts of psychotic buffalos murdering other members of their herd for no apparent reason. There have been innumerable accounts of psychopaths in humans hurting or even murdering other people for no apparent cause. It is mostly inexplicable why all people exhibit behaviors that are irrational, nasty, and predatory against one another. Dark psychology makes an effort to shed some light on topics such as these.

This introduction chapter has covered some of the principles of dark psychology, which is the study of a situation that is rather common in humans but is almost ever addressed. This syndrome is defined by irrational thoughts or behaviors of predation by humans against other people without any acceptable objective or aim, and it is described by those who suffer from it. As was discovered, every human being has a shadow side, and as a result, they have a predatory bent. A cursory examination of history reveals that human beings are capable of being violent, tyrannical, and terrible to one another. On the other hand, these nefarious deeds that mankind have committed have been done on purpose. The shadowy aspect of human nature is often kept in check, but under some circumstances, it is permitted to take control. In dark psychology, the attention is drawn to the very small number of people who are unable to control their violent impulses or ideas and who still choose to act on them.

The Adlerian idea, which asserts that normal people have a tendency to behave in a purposeful manner, has been discussed and described in this chapter. On the other hand, psychopaths do not have any kind of purpose or realistic objective that drives them in the behaviors that they do. The dark singularity, the dark factor, and the black continuum are three essential components of dark psychology that have been analyzed in previous research. The human brain has a region known as the dark singularity, which is home to unadulterated forms of evil. Dark forces are what ultimately entice humans to enter this dimension.

The irrepressible drives to prey on other people are what we refer to as dark elements. When these elements come into play, they take a person farther along the road that leads to the dark singularity. On this scale, humans may be rated anywhere from psychopaths, at one end of the spectrum, to regular people, at the other. When a person commits horrible crimes against other people, they progressively lose their capacity for empathy and compassion, and they grow closer and closer to the singularity. After perpetrating such acts on a consistent basis, they eventually lose all sense of empathy, shame, and compassion, and descend into the shadowy singularity.

In the last section, we discussed the dishonest personalities that are typical of psychopaths. They have the ability to both charm and manipulate others. It is difficult to differentiate a psychopath from a normal individual based just on look or manner of talking. Psychopaths tend to be more sociopathic. Psychopaths are master manipulators who are also excellent planners. Research that led to the conclusion that psychopaths experienced excessive dopamine rewards after they did their terrible deeds is highlighted in the latter portion of this chapter. Because of this, they are willing to accept any and all risks required to accomplish a certain objective. The chapter came to a close by providing an explanation for the unpredictable behavior of psychopaths. The most effective strategy for dealing with them is to fortify one's defenses against their deception in order to prevent falling prey to it..

Chapter Four

The majority of the conclusions that have been drawn regarding psychopaths up to this point in this chapter have been in reference to severe incidents such as murder and arson. However, psychopaths will nonetheless engage in crimes that are not violent and are of a lesser severity. It's possible for psychopaths to be captivating. There is a good chance that a psychopath will not be immediately distinguished from a regular person based on the way that they appear or the way that they communicate. Because of this, the psychopath is able to influence individuals who are trusting of him. Their actual character is only revealed after they have been successful in deceiving or causing damage to other people. A psychopath is emotionally numb and will not experience any remorse or guilt after committing a crime because of this trait.

A study that was carried out at Vanderbilt University came to the conclusion that psychopaths have a dopamine reward system that is overly sensitive. As a result, they will never stop looking for rewards, regardless of the means by which they try to achieve this goal. Because of this, a psychopath who feels fulfilled after successfully deceiving a target will continue to do it to a large number of individuals throughout their life. To put it more simply, a psychopath will engage in any behavior, regardless the dangers, that results in the release of dopamine and brings them some degree of joy.

They are able to maintain their concentration on whatever horrible endeavor they undertake because of the anticipated heightened dopamine reaction. An arsonist will carefully arrange the time and manner in which a home will be set on fire. In addition to this, a serial murderer would methodically plan out the most effective means by which to kill their victims. In the mind of a psychopath, feelings of resentment or any other motivation to inflict damage on others simply do not exist. Dopamine release is the only thing that will make people feel content, and only after it has taken place.

The research that has been done so far in the field of dark psychology has led researchers to the conclusion that the shadowy aspects of humans are unexpected. There are serial murderers who will never hurt their families, while others will begin their sprees by eliminating members of their own families. It is also tough to determine if one is going to follow through and act on whatever malevolent intentions they have. There have been situations in which convicted felons have been released from prison after serving lengthy sentences, only for them to return to their former lives of crime. On the other hand, there have been situations in which convicted felons have made significant progress in their lives after being locked up. Similar to the last point, it is not a given that punishing psychopaths would assist recover their lost sense of rationality, remorse, and responsibility. Therefore, it is in our best interest to learn how to defend oneself against them. The whole of this book will revolve on this topic.

Chapter Five

The last chapter provided an introduction to dark psychology, which is a relatively recent field of research in the field of psychology. In-depth explanations were provided on the disease that causes individuals to display predatory tendencies despite the fact that these instincts are normally latent in healthy people. By contrasting dark psychology with traditional psychology, this chapter will help readers establish a more solid foundation for their comprehension of dark psychology. These two are related but are yet quite different from one another; hence, they are studied independently and the emphasis is placed on various aspects. This chapter will investigate, compare, and contrast the two, with the goal of assisting you in distinguishing between the two. The following subjects will be discussed in it:

What exactly does "normal psychology" entail? What exactly is meant by "dark psychology"?

A contrast between conventional and abnormal psychological approaches Similarities

Differences

The scientific study of the mind and behavior of a normal individual is referred to as "normal psychology," and it makes up the majority of the field of psychology in general. As a result, it places an emphasis on beliefs and actions that are typical or typical of the society as a whole. The discipline of normal psychology consists of a diverse number of subfields due to its numerous facets. Each of these focuses on a different facet of the human mind or behavior as its primary area of study. Nevertheless, these subfields do not yet capture all there is to know about the human mind and behavior in a comprehensive manner. This is due to the fact that psychology as an area of study is relatively recent when compared to other branches of the scientific community. Because of this, the majority of research conducted in the field of psychology has focused on topics that are generally accepted. These may range from typical mental illnesses to emotional states, thought patterns, and behaviors.

Chapter Six

Because of the innovative approaches that they contributed to the field of psychology, William James and Wilhelm Wundt are considered to be its "fathers." Within the field of psychology, the term "functionalism" refers to a strategy that was established by William James in the 1800s to describe the human mind. According to him, the mind was in a perpetual state of searching for new experiences. As a result, the study of psychology has to be approached from the angle of determining what factors led to certain mental processes. A number of years later, Wundt developed a new method for doing psychological research that came to be known as structuralism. If one adopts this point of view, then the study of psychology might be done by introspection. His methodology included asking people who were being studied what was going through their thoughts while they were doing certain activities. This strategy, on the other hand, was unsuccessful since it produced variable outcomes. Wundt was inspired to build a psychology lab in 1875 by the failure of structuralism, and his actions laid the groundwork for the development of contemporary psychology. He distinguished psychology from philosophy because, in his view, it should be approached as a scientific discipline and should include observation, measurement, analysis, and explanation.

Chapter Seven

As a result of Wundt's classification of psychology as a scientific discipline, researchers have discovered that the field encompasses a wide range of topics, including pedagogy, perception, motivation, emotion, personality, mental diseases, and a great deal more. The theoretical explanations that underpin contemporary psychology are extensive. Some psychologists will conduct research on the brain, while others will concentrate on how the brain processes information, how evolution has had an effect on the human brain (which is referred to as "nature"), or how culture and society (which is referred to as "nurture") influences one's behavior or the mental processes that they go through. As was said before, the primary focus of the field of psychology has traditionally been on everyday actions, thoughts, instincts, and perceptions. Because of this, there is a void in the field of research concerning the study of unique and unexpected actions, thoughts, and instincts. This is the void that is filled by dark psychology. [Citation needed]

The concept of "dark psychology" was broken down in some detail in the chapter that came before this one. As a quick review, dark psychology is the study of a latent state that exists in humans and drives them to prey on other people. This condition was discussed in the chapter before this one. It is notable that the majority of individuals are able to inhibit this state, but that some persons are unable to do so and hence display predatory tendencies. The dark continuum is a road that, according to dark psychology, all people may be put on. This path is followed by dark psychology. Following this road will bring you to the world of the black singularity, which is marked by automatic acts of predation. Every time a normal person acts on predatory ideas, they get themselves that much closer to the dark singularity. The term "dark factors" refers to these potentially dangerous ideas.

Chapter Eight

The study of "dark psychology" focuses on the many personalities that might emerge as a consequence of human beings behaving in a predatory manner against other people. The term "psychopath" is the one that is most often used to refer to all of these individuals together in modern culture. A psychopath is described as a person who acts on their predatory tendencies, which leads to behaviors that are callous and insensitive such as torching other people's homes or murdering other people. This definition was presented in chapter 1.

Chapter Nine

The term "dark psychology" refers to a set of attitudes and actions that are often frowned upon, including gratuitous aggressiveness, opportunism, and impulsivity. Psychologists are able to assess how dangerous these behaviors are to other people and what may be done to protect other people from them by doing research on the factors that lead to the behaviors in the first place. The following is a list of personality characteristics that have been compiled by a professor of social psychology at Arizona State University. These characteristics are prevalent in persons who demonstrate dark psychology inclinations.

Narcissism — they may not want to do bodily damage to other people, but they will seek attention in whatever form it may be given to them. As a result of their conduct, which consists of always seeking the approval and admiration of others, they end up being a source of annoyance to everyone around them.

others in order to get something of value for themselves. White collar criminals, sometimes known as Machiavellians, engage in activities like social engineering assaults. An example of this would be Bernard Madoff, who took advantage of his high position at the NYSE to scam investors out of millions of dollars.

Psychopaths have a propensity to be cruel, heartless, impulsive, manipulative, and grandiose in their thinking and behavior. They are often ready to physically damage people in order to experience the delights that come with satisfying their impulses of predation. They do not consider the potential repercussions of their acts and do not care about the people whose lives are negatively affected as a result of their activities. Because psychopaths are often socially proficient, they pose a threat to their victims because they are able to create positive initial impressions with their victims and then go on to damage them when they are least expecting it.

People that take pleasure in inflicting pain on others are known as sadists. Sadists are more likely to choose careers that put them in positions of power, where they may inflict pain on others with little risk of being held accountable by the law. Such professions include those in the police force, the military, and even those in leadership roles in religious organizations, such as the priests.

There are just a few parallels that can be drawn between the two. The most important similarity is that both are subfields of psychology in general. The field of psychology is expansive, and it includes both abnormal and healthy forms of the field. Therefore, if normal psychology did not already exist, there could be no room for dark psychology. If philosophy and psychology had not been separated out into their own fields, there is a good likelihood that there would not be any specific concentration on dark psychology as an area of study today. In addition, dark psychology and traditional psychology have a lot of similarities in the methods that they use to investigate the mind and behavior of humans. This is due to the fact that they are reliant on scientific research procedures that are designed to achieve outcomes that have a theoretical justification or explanation. Beyond this, there aren't really too many more things that are comparable between the two.

Chapter Ten

Differences

Chapter Eleven

There is a world of difference between abnormal and healthy psychological thought. Dark psychology, on the other hand, focuses on particular anomalies of the human brain that make a person more likely to prey on others, as opposed to the more traditional field of psychology, which studies the general workings of the brain as well as individual behavior. Therefore, traditional psychology will center its attention on the average members of society, but dark psychology would concentrate on the minority of outliers. It was said in the first chapter that 99 percent of human behavior is purposeful and logical, whereas

1 percent of human behavior is involuntary and irrational. The vast majority of people—some 99 percent—fit neatly into the category of "typical," hence the focus of normal psychology will be on these individuals. For instance, traditional psychology would be interested in discovering the reasons behind why people experience depression given how frequent it is. However, conventional psychology will not be able to provide exhaustive explanations for the aberrations that cause individuals to commit crimes such as arson and serial murder. Dark psychology specialists are the ones who are responsible for this area of psychology.

Chapter Twelve

Dark psychology focuses on a part of the human brain that has the potential to make people behave in an uncontrollable manner similar to that of predators. Because this area is present in all individuals but dormant in the majority of them, it is an essential component of psychological study. Let's take a look at Sigmund Freud's dissection of the human mind in order to have a better understanding of the subtle differences that exist between traditional psychology and dark psychology.

Chapter Thirteen

In the early 20th century, Sigmund Freud developed a topographical model of the mind that was intended to shed light on the composition of the brain. His model was that of an iceberg, which is shown in the following figure:

Chapter Fourteen

Figure 1: An iceberg

According to Freud, the portion of the brain that is conscious and responsible for the mental activity one is consciously aware of is only the tip of the iceberg. This is the topic that students majoring in normal psychology will focus on since it is composed of ideas and perceptions that typical individuals have. When working with a client, a certified psychotherapist will concentrate on the client's conscious brain in order to assist the client in improving their life, enhancing their cognitive skills, and developing coping mechanisms.

The subconscious is the layer of one's mind that lies just below the water's surface, and it is made up of things that individuals are consciously ignorant of but that may be retrieved from their brains. This is where memories of things like people, locations, and events will be kept, among other things. Because everything that is stored in this region of the brain can be brought back to the conscious state, conventional psychology can still make sense of it.

Chapter Fifteen

On the other hand, the greater portion of the iceberg that is submerged under the ocean is what Freud referred to as the unconscious. This is what contains things that we are not aware of and may never become aware of in the future. Freud believed that the unconscious was the location of more primal impulses and wants. Nevertheless, both the awareness and the subconscious work together to suppress these desires. The unconscious has an effect on human conduct, as well as sensations and influences. However, humans are unable to decipher the information that is kept in this portion of the mind. Through cognitive and social psychology, normal psychology delves into the realm of the unconscious to investigate some parts of it. The many ways in which people's ideas, perceptions, and behaviors may be changed as a result of understanding and applying the discoveries discovered regarding this region of the brain.

Chapter Sixteen

If you want to learn how to control someone's thinking, one activity you may attempt is to play rock-paper-scissors with a buddy while simultaneously trying to plant a concept in their unconscious mind. You may easily do this by just representing the rock, paper, and scissors with your own hands at the beginning of each round. Because the picture of the scissors is the final one to be implanted into their unconscious, it is quite probable that they will try to win against the scissors. Even before the game begins, you will have already changed their brain processes such that they think in a certain way. In the movie "Inception," released in 2010, Leonardo DiCaprio plays the role of Dom Cobb, who asserts that once an idea has been implanted in the unconscious, it is very difficult to remove it. It becomes a hardy parasite. This makes sense from a psychology perspective given that the unconscious mind has a significant impact on even the smallest, most inconsequential choices that you make on a daily basis.

On the other hand, Freud proposed that there are some sinister wants that, in order to prevent them from ever materializing, must be repressed and buried deep within the unconscious. These wants are not the center of normal psychology, but they are the foundation of dark psychology. Normal psychology ignores them. This is the location of the predatory instincts, which include things like irrational wants, immoral drives, and aggressive intentions. Normal psychology will be

concerned with the normal parts of the unconscious, but will have only a basic knowledge of
the illogical and involuntary drives that lay dormant in this region of the brain. On the other
hand, dark psychology will not place a significant
amount of emphasis on other aspects of the unconscious other than those that lead to illogical
and out of control thoughts and actions. At this
point, the divide between abnormal and healthy
psychology may be clearly seen.

Chapter Seventeen

Conclusion

By contrasting it with traditional psychology, this chapter has contributed to a deeper and more comprehensive knowledge of dark psychology. The concept of normal psychology has been broken down, and the evolution of psychology as a distinct academic discipline has been analyzed, all the way from the time of the ancient philosophers to the present day and the area of contemporary psychology. In addition, a short discussion on dark psychology was included in chapter 1, as was stated there. After that, a contrast between dark psychology and traditional psychology was drawn. The few points of similarity between the two have been broken down and discussed. The remainder of the chapter examines the contrasts that exist between the two disciplines. The topographical model of the human mind that Sigmund Freud developed has been used widely to describe how psychology and neuroscience approach different aspects of the human brain in their respective areas of concentration. As a result, the knowledge of dark psychology has been expanded as a result of this chapter since it has clarified the areas of study that are included in it and how it contrasts with traditional psychology.

Chapter Eighteen

History to demonstrate that those who were able to exert influence over their surroundings had always been at an advantage in the game of natural selection. The first humans were able to make it through life in the jungle by adapting to their surroundings and creating tools for hunting, shelters to stay warm and protect themselves from other animals, and weapons to defend themselves. However, manipulation did not cease with early man, nor has it been confined to people influencing the planet in order to prosper as a species. Rather, manipulation has been going on from the beginning of time. The ability to manipulate, which is a kind of the predatory instinct, has been covertly transferred into the contemporary world and is now being utilized by people against one another.

When manipulating individuals, it is common practice to focus on exploiting their sensory organs as well as their behavioral characteristics. As was said before, researchers in dark psychology have noticed that it may be difficult to differentiate between a psychopath, sociopath, and narcissist based just on a person's physical appearance alone. These distinct groups of individuals that prey routinely on other humans are intertwined throughout the fabric of the society. They are, among other things, our physicians, attorneys, and police officers, as well as our parents and children. They will often resort to manipulating people, which is one of the tools they have at their disposal, in order to do damage to others or to ensure that things go their way. Depending on the method that the manipulator uses, it may be difficult to identify manipulation. Depending on the circumstances or the effect that you want, you may carry it out either discretely or openly. In this chapter, we will review a variety of covert and overt manipulation tactics, including the following:

Chapter Nineteen

Manipulation behind the scenes

The most difficult kind of manipulation to detect is covert manipulation, which masquerades as movements that are well-intentioned or innocent at first. The manipulator utilizes these covert strategies in the hopes that the victim would unwittingly into their traps, which will allow them to exert easy control over them. There is a good chance that those who are being controlled will not let on to their victims that they are being manipulated. They will have the false impression that their behaviors are the result of their own free will, despite the fact that this is not the case. Techniques of covert manipulation include the following, among others:

Chapter Twenty

Victimhood

The manipulator would prey on their targets by portraying the role of a victim to exaggerated challenges of personal nature such as health complications, employment issues, or difficulties in their relationships. This strategy is used to immediately evoke compassion from a target in order to achieve one's goals. The target will eventually give in to your pleas for sympathy and agree to provide some assistance. Since the manipulator takes on the role of a helpless and vulnerable person, the victim will feel compelled to assist in whatever way they can because they believe they are doing the right thing. The manipulator will then be in a position to ask the target for whatever they want, which is a perfect opportunity for them.

Because there are three people involved, victimhood is conceptualized in psychology as "The Victim Triangle." These parties are the victim, the rescuer, and the persecutor. When one person in the triangle assumes a position, you will unintentionally take on the character of the other person. In any event, the manipulator acts the part of the victim, points the finger of guilt at an aggressor, and coerces you to play the part of the savior. For instance, the manipulator may claim that his financial difficulties are the result of a fatal disease. In the event that he or she subsequently discloses that they are unable to pay their rent or buy food, it will be required of you to play the part of the savior. If well planned, it will make you feel sensitive, and you will want to provide your assistance. However, this approach is most successful in the short term due to the fact that the person attempting to help the victim quickly recognizes that none of the aid provided has had any impact on improving their situation.

Chapter Twenty-One

Gaslighting

Chapter Twenty-Two

Another kind of covert psychological manipulation, this one involves the manipulator attempting to cast doubt on the target's memory, perception, or even sanity in order to gain control over them. This strategy is often used by sociopaths and narcissists since it is successful over the course of time and gives them further power to mistreat the people they are targeting. The purpose of the manipulator is to guarantee that the target will doubt themselves and will be forced to question their decisions as well as their mental stability. Because of this, the victim will begin to believe that they are unable to make their own choices, and as a result, they will be forced to become dependant on their abuser. In order for this degree of manipulation to take place, it is necessary for the manipulator to have control over the environment in which the target is operating. As a result, it is not difficult to use it in a variety of settings and contexts, including motherhood, slavery, marriages, religious cults, dictatorships, the military, and prisons, amongst others. The following steps are included in the process of gaslighting:

i. Keeping information from the target in order to increase their vulnerability to being manipulated; this occurs when the target has less knowledge than the manipulator. The manipulator will assume control of the information sources that their victim has access to, and they will use this power to their advantage. He has a variety of ingenious methods at his disposal to deter victims from aggressively pursuing information from other sources. For instance, a member of a cult may get instructions from the cult leader to abstain from watching television or logging into social networking sites because the leader believes that doing so would cause their minds to become corrupted. As a result, the head of the cult functions as the members of the cult's primary information resource. This strategy has a good chance of succeeding under authoritarian regimes or penal institutions with restricted access to outside information. For instance, the internet in countries like North Korea is heavily controlled, which means that citizens of such nations are unable to access websites that provide information that is in opposition to what they have been led to think by their government. When the sole source of information is the abuser, it is relatively simple to mislead the victims into feeling that only the abuser is correct or knows what is best for them.

This is especially true when the abuser is the only source of information.

ii. Twisting the facts to fit the narrative of the manipulator - An abuser will be stingy with information and will only reveal what is relevant to their story. They will also alter the facts to demonstrate that they have been correct the whole time and that the victim has been in the wrong. The manipulator will alter the facts in such a way as to cast doubt on the victim's understanding of the situation. Any information that the victim has that runs counter to what the manipulator asserts will likewise be the focus of the manipulator's attention. The "truth" that the manipulator conveys to the victim will eventually cause the victim to grow reliant on it.

Chapter Twenty-Three

iii. Exerting Influence On the Victim and Their Environment The manipulator will try to exert influence over the victim and their surrounding environment. In order to do this, the victim is first isolated from their family and friends. These are the first places of contact that might cause the victim's views and conduct to shift or even be called into question. The manipulator will have complete control over the victim's thoughts and behavior while the victim is alone and isolated from other people.

Psychologists feel that gaslighting is often more successful when employed against women, despite the fact that it may be used against both men and women. This is because there is a widespread cultural expectation that women should behave in a subservient manner. Someone else will have an easier time getting them to question their own viewpoints, beliefs, and recollections as a result of this.

Chapter Twenty-Four

Excessive reliance on factual and statistical evidence

By portraying oneself as someone who is very informed, you may quickly establish mental control over another person. This can be a very effective tactic. To give the impression that they are knowledgeable in a subject matter(s), some manipulators like engaging in intellectual bullying. As a result, they will make use of purported facts or figures, neither of which the victim is aware of. An authority in psychology in the 21st century named Mike Alvin claims that if you present information in an engaging manner, you can convince people to believe whatever you say. Sadly, this is not accurate since the specific psychology expert being referred to in the quotation does not exist, and neither does the quote itself. You have probably seen that the average reader or listener will just accept quotations from purported sources as unquestionable facts. They are not going to put much effort into verifying the accuracy of what they have read or heard. This is something that manipulators use to their advantage in order to convince their targets of various facts and data, some of which may not even be genuine, in order to get an intellectual edge over them. When a target often hears a manipulator dishing out facts and numbers, the target will quickly begin to believe that the manipulator is extremely informed due of the repeated behavior. As a consequence of this, the manipulator will exert their authority over the target and turn them into a victim.

Chapter Twenty-Five

As soon as the manipulator has established a reputation for intellectual superiority, he or she will need less effort to advance a covert agenda since the targets will quickly accept it as a result of the manipulator's intellectual superiority. When they wish to push for their items, marketers may sometimes employ this strategy. They are able to obtain an audience with the market and promote their own agendas merely by mentioning certain facts, even if the facts are not correct or do not affect their goods. In the field of psychology, the term "manipulator" refers to a person who takes advantage of their elevated position in the hierarchy of intellects to prey on their victims by asking for favors.

Chapter Twenty-Six

Time constraint - urgency

When you don't give someone enough time to think about something, you have the highest chance of getting them to agree to something they would not typically do. The manipulators are masters at applying time pressure to the targets in order to force them to make judgments before the targets are even ready. This results in tension, and since there is so little time to carefully consider one's response, it is easier to just give in to the demands of the aggressor.

The effects of time constraints on decision making were investigated in a research carried out by Yang, Goodie, Hall, and Wu. They stated that the purpose of a decision maker should be to make the best selections possible while experiencing the least amount of mental strain possible. According to their results, it was unmistakable that an increase in the amount of time pressure led to an increase in the amount of risk taking while making decisions. This was particularly true for actions that resulted in good advantages for the individuals making the decisions. The conclusion that can be drawn from this research is that an individual's propensity to take risks grows as the time constraint associated with a decision-making process is increased. Due to the fact that they do not have a complete understanding of the option they are selecting or the commitment they are making, they will therefore make more dangerous selections.

Chapter Twenty-Seven

It is possible for manipulators to utilize the sense of urgency to convince their targets to agree to specific conditions even before the targets are aware of the implications that are involved in the situation. Later on, the targets become victims of the predatory demands made by the manipulator, and because they have already locked themselves into contracts, they have no choice but to comply with the demands.

Chapter Twenty-Eight

The treatment of silence

Chapter Twenty-Nine

The use of silence as a kind of psychological coercion is one strategy. It is frequent practice in partnerships, particularly in marriages if one of the parties is a manipulator, and it is especially prevalent in abusive relationships. The manipulator will consciously refrain from interacting in any kind of communication with the person they are controlling. The goal of the manipulator is to sow seeds of uncertainty and doubt in the mind of the person they are trying to control. The person who is on the receiving end of the silent treatment will suffer significantly as they begin to experience very unpleasant feelings. They experience feelings of inadequacy, worthlessness, separation, and isolation as a result. They get the impression that the offender is implicitly blaming themselves for what happened to them. They are also unable to fathom what they did incorrectly to deserve such a response from others.

Chapter Thirty

The victims have the impression that they are required to reestablish connection by whatever means necessary. The manipulator now has leeway to ask for or demand specific favors as a result of this. For instance, if the manipulator requests money from the victim, the victim would cheerfully give the manipulator money, even if it is in excess of what was asked for. As long as there is anything the manipulator wants from the victim and they will not accept the victim's refusal as a response, the manipulator will continue to use the silent treatment approach to continue leeching off of the victim.

Chapter Thirty-One

Guilt trip

Chapter Thirty-Two

In this kind of emotional manipulation, a target is made to feel guilty in order to accomplish the desired effect on their emotions. These emotions of guilt may then be utilized by the manipulator to manipulate the conduct of the target and make them submit to the will of the manipulator. As with the silent treatment, guilt trips are most prevalent in romantic partnerships and, at first glance, the victim may believe that they are safe, but in the long run, they may be quite damaging. When chatting to someone or texting, a manipulator may attempt to incorporate a few phrases or questions that will make the target feel guilty.

This approach is often employed in communication. Those who engage in the usage of guilt trips are often oblivious to the harm that they do. For instance, a mother who does things like telling her children that she had to work for twelve hours straight just to put food on the table as a form of discouragement whenever her children ask her to buy them toys or pay for trips is not aware of the long-term consequences of doing things like that. They will have the immediate effect of discouraging the children from requesting money or other favors from the adults. However, these words are like a slow poison that, over time, will result in emotional distance or anger between the parties involved. When it comes to marriage, manipulative partners might use guilt trips as a way to indirectly put pressure on their partners to give them favors via the use of indirect pressure. They will force them to agree to every request they have by subtly suggesting that they are guilty of anything in their comments.

Chapter Thirty-Three

Manipulation in plain sight

Some people who manipulate are not distinct in the predatory actions that they engage in. They will thus verbally and physically assault victims in an open manner merely to get their way. The following is an example of the methods that they employ:

Chapter Thirty-Four

Voicing of distressing feelings and emotions

This is a hostile form of manipulation that seeks to instill fear in the person who is the target of the tactic. It is possible to accomplish this by using forceful body language or by raising one's voice in order to make it abundantly clear that the manipulator demands immediate compliance with any request or command that is given. For instance, new members of a disciplined force are frequently subjected to verbal abuse at the hands of their instructors, who yell at them. They are also not permitted to respond unless specifically asked to do so. The majority of the commands are going to be yelled out, and the recruits are going to quickly follow them. Outside of the military, the same tactic is utilized in families in which children are subjected to abuse at the hands of their parents. A parent will use a loud or intimidating voice when giving a child even the most basic of instructions, such as telling the child to complete some chores. The most favorable conditions for carrying out this kind of manipulation are when the target possesses fewer powers than the manipulator. They hope to instill a sense of dread and extreme discomfort in their targets, causing them to quickly cave in to their demands.

Chapter Thirty-Five

Deception

When it serves their purposes, manipulators are skilled liars who are able to twist the truth in any way that benefits them. They are willing to tell lies in order to advance their goals, even when there are obvious facts that contradict what they claim to be the case. In addition to this, manipulators are notorious for contradicting what they previously stated. They are able to make pledges in order to gain some sort of benefit from their targets; however, when it comes time for them to fulfill the promise, they will claim that they never made any pledges at all. Even conversations that have already taken place can be twisted by manipulators to give their targets the impression that they are the ones in the wrong. The goal of these efforts to twist the facts is to make the target of the manipulation feel bad for challenging the manipulator.

Chapter Thirty-Six

However, it is not hard at all for the person who is the target of the manipulation to realize that they are being deceived, particularly if they have access to facts or recordings in which the manipulator makes promises. It is common practice for manipulators to use deception as a bait and switch tactic, in which they promise one thing in exchange for another favor. The target complies with the manipulator's request and patiently waits for them to keep their end of the bargain, only to discover that the manipulator has lied their way out of the situation. Targets can also be lied to about the manipulators' true identities by manipulators. After that, it is much simpler for the targets to be duped into believing that they are interacting with genuine individuals. In the field of cybersecurity, there is a specific form of attack known as social engineering that has proven to be effective against highly protected businesses. It requires the use of fictitious identities by the cybercriminals, as well as direct communication with employees of the targeted company. After that, they are able to make demands for things such as money, login credentials, sensitive files, and other favors. There have been a number of instances of hacking or theft of funds by hackers that have resulted in losses to various organizations. In 2013, Yahoo was the target of an attack that involved the use of social engineering, which resulted in the stolen account details of nearly three billion users. This should be sufficient evidence to show that one of the most effective methods of manipulation is lying.

Chapter Thirty-Seven

Punishment

Manipulative punishments are frequently the cause of abusive relationships that last for a long period of time. When all else fails, a manipulator will resort to hurting their victim physically in order to get what they want. There have been multiple reports of sexual abuse spanning multiple decades, in which the victims have been physically harmed and threatened with further harm if they report their afflictions to law enforcement agencies or the general public. These reports have come from victims who have been subjected to both verbal and physical abuse. There have also been reports of abusive parenting, in which parents have been accused of mistreating, beating, or otherwise inflicting physical or emotional harm on their children for an extended period of time. This method of manipulation is frequently used in situations in which the manipulator has a significant degree of control over the victim's movements and the victim's interactions with other people.

Chapter Thirty-Eight

The victims are left with both physical and emotional scars as a direct result of the punishments, which has the effect of making them feel fragile and defenseless in the face of their manipulators. Sometimes as a result of this, an unusual relationship develops between the two parties, and the victim ends up developing feelings of attachment to the manipulator. There was a news article that was published in The New Yorker that detailed how girls who had been kidnapped in Nigeria by a terrorist group known as Boko Haram were rescued, only to go back to the terrorists shortly after their rescue. The article focused on how the girls had been kidnapped by Boko Haram. A connection had been forged between them and their captors, who had subjected them to torture, rape, and murder for petty reasons such as refusing to watch the executions carried out by the members of the group. In spite of the fact that they are aware of this fact, they are more willing to put their lives in danger in order to return to the woods and reunite with the terrorists. Therefore, punishment is a method of manipulation that is used over the long term, and the more a victim is subjected to it, the closer they will become with their abuser.

Chapter Thirty-Nine

Projection

Toxic environments can be created around manipulators, but they can always find someone else to blame for the problems they cause. This is a defense mechanism that psychopaths and narcissists utilize in order to shift any feelings of guilt or responsibility onto other people. They will attribute their unfavorable qualities to another person or blame that individual for their unfavorable or even potentially harmful behavior. There is a good chance that the targets are compassionate people who will agree with the projections made by the manipulator. They will eventually come to the realization that it is they, and not the manipulators, who are the source of the problem. It's common for the parents of people who commit crimes or who become terrorists to experience this phenomenon, in which they blame themselves for the actions of their children. If a criminal takes something and then turns around and blames his or her poor upbringing on the parent, the parent will almost always accept responsibility for the theft. Additionally, the parent will experience feelings of responsibility for all of the illegal acts that their child has carried out. This tactic typically involves the victim's emotions, and as a result, the victim begins to take on the mental and emotional burdens of the manipulator.

Chapter Forty

Conclusion

For all of human history, manipulation has been an inherent part of the human experience. It is the factor that has contributed to his success in dominating and thriving in his environment. However, there are some people who will manipulate others in order to take advantage of them. This chapter has discussed the two categories of manipulation techniques that are commonly used, covert and overt. These techniques can be broken down further into subcategories. It is difficult to detect covert manipulation, which may appear benign to the person being manipulated. In overt manipulation, the manipulator's intentions are not hidden, and they prey directly on the person they are trying to control. Victimhood, gas lighting, excessive use of facts and statistics, time pressure, the silent treatment, guilt trips, and guilt trips are some of the covert manipulation techniques that are discussed. The expression of negative emotions, deception, punishment, and projection are all examples of overt manipulation techniques that have been brought up in this discussion. The end result of all of these different techniques of manipulation is the same: the perpetrators of the manipulation prey on their victims, with varying degrees of success in the short term and the long term. term.

Chapter Forty-One

Reciprocation

Hatred breeds more hatred, according to a well-known proverb, and similarly, violence breeds more violence. The underlying implication of statements like these is that people will always react similarly to one another. If they are treated violently, they will reply in like with more violence. On the other hand, if you treat them kindly and favorably, they will treat you kindly and favorably in return. The following is how the process of reciprocation works:

1. You award a favor

2. You ask the recipient of the favor for another favor. 3. The recipient of the first favor feels obligated to you.

4. The request has been fulfilled.

The practice of reciprocation is used more often than meets the eye. One is encouraged, beginning in infancy, to reply to any act of generosity with a "thank you" in order to demonstrate appreciation. That is a type of return for the favor. Politicians will make an effort to look altruistic and concerned with the lives of residents during electioneering seasons because they want voter support in exchange for their good deeds and humanitarian gestures. It has been noted that certain pharmaceutical corporations donate free equipment or other gifts to hospitals, and that as a result, physicians prescribe patients medications that are manufactured by these businesses.

When it comes to winning the acquiescence of a sensible individual, reciprocation is one of the most successful methods. However, it will only be successful if the target is presented with something that they consider to be of great value. When they have finished consuming it, a sense of obligation begins to take hold of them. One will say "thank you" in response to even the smallest of acts of kindness, such as holding open the door to an elevator so that another person may enter. When you do someone a favor, like paying their tab at a restaurant or bar, you will keep them in debt, and they will be eager to repay you with a much larger favor if you do it again. If you express that you need assistance in any way, they will most likely volunteer to provide it when asked.

In order to ensnare their prey, manipulators take advantage of the fact that people are subject to an overwhelming law of reciprocation. They will act as if they care and be willing to provide money, presents, or free services in order to give the impression that they are generous. However, they will have prepared in advance how they would take advantage of individuals who have accepted their gifts or aid and will have a strategy for doing so. Simply by accepting the bait presented in the form of a free gift, manipulators might set in motion a chain reaction consisting of asking for favors from another person. This will continue until the sensation of being obliged to them no longer exists.

It has been shown that reciprocation is effective even on a worldwide scale. It is common practice for superpower nations to provide less developed nations with aid in the form of money, food, or even military assistance free of charge. However, the same countries will swiftly overwhelm the country they are purportedly helping with low-cost exports, or they will begin taking away the country's natural resources without any bargaining. Therefore, reciprocation is very effective at any size and is associated with high success rates.

Chapter Forty-Two

Obligation

The "responsibility to rescue" is a subject that is often covered in depth in legal education programs. In nations where this kind of tort law is applied, a person may be held legally accountable for failing to come to the rescue of another individual who, if they were not saved, might suffer serious injury or even death. There are a number of commitments that each and every logical human being is expected to uphold. These responsibilities may be contractual, ethical, legal, or even religious in nature. Helpdesk officers, who are responsible for providing assistance to customers or other members of staff, are one group of individuals who encounter the impacts of contractual responsibilities in a direct and personal manner. They are often insulted, but all they can do is gently ask callers to be patient while they provide the help since they are legally bound to do so. Despite this, they are forced to deal with the situation. In a variety of different methods, manipulators attempt to take advantage of an individual's feeling of duty. They could introduce themselves to you as victims in need of assistance.

There have been instances of carjackings in which the victims were innocently helping a stranded "couple" on the side of the road who had a flat tire before they were taken hostage. The manipulators are skilled at creating the situations that would vividly recall one's moral responsibility to aid another person. They may, among other things, appear to be destitute, disabled, or abandoned in order to get free money or other resources from individuals who are unaware of their deception. The cultivation of the target is necessary for the use of obligation as a method of persuasion to be successful. People who were raised in societies in which it is obligatory to help people in need are at a high risk of falling prey to manipulators who manipulate the concept of duty. Because of this, the percentage of times that this strategy is successful is directly proportional to the degree to which the target feels obligated.

Chapter Forty-Three

Concession

There are situations in which the most effective method to achieve victory is to concede an initial defeat. There is a strategy that debaters use to disarm their opponents called "agreeing with the opponent only to finish off by pounding a strong point of dissent." This is a maneuver that debaters employ to disarm their opponents. This maneuver first reduces the impact of an argument made by an opponent, which then makes way for one to raise a more compelling point of their own. When it comes to the art of persuasion, manipulators are constantly seeking for methods to soothe stressful situations or disagreements with the people they are trying to influence so that they may reach agreements in which they stand to profit the most. Because the two sides to any contract will both be attempting to further their own interests, heated times are to be anticipated during the negotiation process. The manipulator's only goal is to benefit themselves at the expense of the target, but they need to avoid becoming involved in any substantial disputes that may compromise their plans and prevent them from being successful. They do this by giving the targets the opportunity to make the initial move in negotiating a transaction, only to have the manipulator agree to it and then add additional stipulations from which they will gain.

The manipulator's goal is to convince the target that a sweetheart bargain or agreement with long-term repercussions is in their best interest. The manipulator will let the target to make the first offer or request, and then they will comply with whatever was proposed. The manipulator, on the other hand, will continue to tack on some further conditions or ask for yet another favor in exchange. The manipulator will have provided himself or herself a platform to gain what they actually required from the other party if, before agreeing to the requests of the target, they agree to the demands that the target is making.

Concerns have recently been raised over the terms of the loans that a powerful nation in Asia has been providing to other nations in Asia with the intention of luring them into a cycle of unsustainable debt. For example, the nation consented to provide Sri Lanka with a loan, but in exchange, it gained control of Sri Lanka's port for a term of one hundred years. The loan arrangement had specific clauses that made it possible for the port to be seized as collateral, and those terms came back to haunt Sri Lanka when the country was unable to make its monthly payments on the loan. Although Sri Lanka was granted the financing it asked, the loaner's primary objective was to gain control of an important port located along a trade route. Employers are able to get an edge via the usage of concession when it comes to the recruiting process. Some companies may agree to offer the job candidate the wage that they have asked, but they will also come up with stipulations for the contract that are on the verge of being considered slavery. When one side is under pressure or has less influence than the other, concession may be a strong tool. Because of this, it is much simpler to take advantage of them. The effectiveness of this method is highly dependent on the manipulator's capacity for patience, despite the fact that it is fairly successful.

Chapter Forty-Four

Scarcity

When it comes to commerce, the prices of commodities tend to adhere to the standard pattern in which they are determined by the competing forces of demand and supply in a given market. Because of this scarcity, the prices of goods tend to be rather high. In the art of persuasion, it is possible to manufacture a sense of scarcity in order to induce a target to agree to terms that are not favorable in the first place. Deals of this kind will inevitably lead to manipulators taking advantage of the parties involved. One-day promotions and limited offers are a frequent strategy used by marketers to entice customers to make purchases throughout the shopping process. Since of this, a buyer will consider it sensible to acquire an item during a 1-day sale because there is a possibility that they will never have another opportunity to buy the item with such an offer. The same logic applies to the process of persuasion. It is intended for the targets to get the impression that they are going to miss out on something significant. Because of this, they will respond quickly and be encouraged to do so in order to avoid missing out.

The majority of the time, manipulators do this by increasing the sense of urgency. People who are given an extended period of time to think about a decision will either come to the conclusion that the option they are considering is not worthwhile or they will put off making the decision. As a result of the fact that manipulators do not want their targets to discover the cons hidden in the offers they provide, they will constantly attempt to speed up the decision-making process. For instance, those who have been taken advantage of by pyramid schemes would have entered into "get rich fast" agreements after giving themselves very little time to truly consider about what they were committing to. This is because they were promised that they could become wealthy very quickly.

Bitcoin, a cryptocurrency that was marketed to many people with the promise that the money they put in it would fast expand, was one of the most popular investments in 2017. In 2017, there was a high level of enthusiasm for Bitcoin. The price of one coin of a cryptocurrency shot up significantly as a direct result of the growing popularity of the cryptocurrency. In August of 2017, the price was at $4,000 a coin; however, the sudden increase in demand caused the price to skyrocket, and it reached $19000 just five months later. At this time, individuals were being encouraged to purchase Bitcoins as quickly as possible, despite the fact that the prices were very high, on the grounds that the cryptocurrency would continue to increase in value. Unfortunately, the value of the currency was swiftly pounded down to below $2,000 later in 2018, causing a great deal of financial hardship for a great number of individuals. This may or may not be related to manipulation, but it is a clear demonstration of how the promise of immediate returns readily persuades individuals to make short-term investments in things with which they are only somewhat aware.

If the people being targeted give in to the high-pressure atmosphere that is being created for them by their manipulators, then the scarcity tactic has a good chance of being successful. Fear of losing out will force the targets to impulsively agree to such transactions, and by the time they understand that they have been conned and are just being preyed on, it is always too late for them to do anything about it.

Chapter Forty-Five

Dedication and perseverance are required.

The majority of individuals are quite good at keeping their word when it comes to previous commitments. If they are offered with the same alternatives as before, it is probable that they will continue to make the same decisions that they did previously. This is due to the fact that the human brain makes every effort to choose the route that requires the least amount of effort. It does not need to reprocess the data in order to arrive at a conclusion; rather, it only verifies the conclusion it reached before. It has been shown that the mere act of asking individuals if they would come out to vote leads to a high follow-through percentage for those who indicate they would vote. This is the case for those people who say they will vote. They are aware that they have already promised to vote, thus in order to fulfill this obligation, they will need to physically go to the polling place and cast their vote.

Individuals may be easily manipulated into making promises, and when it comes to following through with consistency, manipulators will not hesitate to take advantage of the people they have manipulated. In the context of auctions, it is standard practice for competitors to strive to outbid one another to the point that the price they offer is higher than the item's current market worth. Each of them has indicated that they want to purchase the item that is now up for auction and will endeavor to win the item by placing a greater bid before the other bidder does. People who have a problem with gambling will often gamble until they have lost all of their money, in the hope that they will eventually win something.

In most cases, prior experiences serve as the foundation for consistency. For instance, compulsive gamblers will have prior experiences of winning, and they will strive to accomplish the same level of success in each and every game that they play. A con job known as "Business Email Compromise" has been floating around recently. This name was given to it by the FBI. Hackers will impersonate the email address of an executive employee and then use that account to give commands to lower-level employees when they do this. The vast majority of these orders consist of exchanging information or credentials and completing immediate financial transactions. In the beginning, the hackers may ask for something of very modest value, such as the URL of a customer's website. As soon as the junior staff has submitted the response, they will have made a tiny commitment to replying to the executive via the counterfeit email. After there, the hackers are able to make audacious demands, such as the transfer of dollars or the provision of passwords to critical computer systems. Instead than asking the junior employees why their "executive" needs access credentials, it is more consistent to just provide them to them and not have them explain why they need it.

Luring the targets into making tiny commitments is the most important step in successfully manipulating them via dedication and consistency. Because of this very little commitment, the target will be extremely receptive to any follow-up demands that seem to be in line with what they have already committed to. Even something as simple as a welcome may be used by manipulators as a springboard for taking advantage of others. They should just approach a target and inquire directly ""Hey there, how are you doing?" If the target claims to be successful, the manipulator will respond by saying something along the lines of "Great, since I am not and I could use your aid."" In this scenario, the manipulator will have gained the target's attention by virtue of the target's assertion that they are doing well. They have elevated themselves to a position where they have a moral obligation to assist individuals who are not in the same position as them just by providing this answer. The least that can be expected of them is to provide an attentive ear when the manipulator begins explaining their predicament and making a request for assistance. After then, it is possible to solicit substantial donations from them in order to support the manipulator. They will feel forced to help in order to put a stop to this obligation since consistency requires them to do so.

As can be seen, two of the most successful methods of persuasion are being consistent and being committed to what you say. A commitment trap may even be set up with something as innocuous as a reaction to a hello. However, since the targets grow more wary after being exploited by the strategy, its odds of succeeding in future attempts are significantly reduced. However, in other instances, the targets are unaware that they are victims, and as a result, they will continue to fall for new promises for a considerable amount of time.

Chapter Forty-Six

Liking

The majority of individuals value the perception that they are loved. They also have a propensity to like back those who already like them. This strategy is used often in the field of marketing. When meeting a prospective customer for the first time, marketers will do their best to seem knowledgeable and put out an image of themselves as nice individuals. Nevertheless, this should not be interpreted to suggest that salesmen who do not conform to the conventional standards of attractiveness do not have the ability to close deals. This is due to the fact that an appeal to the prospective customer's sense of liking will be made in order to sway their decision. The marketers will work to create an environment in which the consumer feels valued and validated, increasing the likelihood that the customer will make a purchase.

The same script is utilized throughout the process of manipulation.

Targets are often lead to think, amongst other things, that they are beautiful, knowledgeable, intelligent, careful, or socially recognized persons. This is one of the more common forms of psychological manipulation. It doesn't matter what kind of validation is employed as long as it brings joy to the target audience. This stimulates the reverse like process, in which the person who has been validated will like the manipulator again, or at least appear to like them. On the other hand, there are also instances in which the people being targeted do not place any importance on or care about the approval of other people. As a result, the manipulators need to seek validation for themselves by endeavoring to engage in activities that would appeal to the target audience. For instance, a manipulator may visit the home or business of someone who is passionate about art and bring along an old piece of carving. The artist will have a strong emotional connection to that object, and as a result, they will be impressed by the manipulator and almost instantly begin to like them. When a victim has been manipulated into liking the manipulator, taking advantage of that target is simple. Because the charmed targets provide the manipulators with an audience, they are in a better position to ask for favors, and there is a good probability that their requests will be granted.

This kind of persuasion is a challenge on many levels. In most cases, it is utilized on particular targets that the manipulator deems to be of value to them. The results will be different for everyone since it all depends on how well the blindfold of validation holds up on the target. However, if the manipulator is able to delight the target in an even greater way, it will be possible to increase the efficacy. There are strategies that may be used, such as positive reinforcements, gestures, and tone, in order to maintain the connection between the manipulator and the target for a sufficient amount of time in order for the mission to be successful.

Chapter Forty-Seven

Evidence from society

Herd behavior is a term that may be used to describe the typical behavior of groups of animals. When one animal (or person) in a certain setting adopts the behavior that it sees exhibited by other animals (or people) in that environment, this phenomenon is known as social proof. We have a tendency to laugh at jokes even if we do not think them humorous merely because other people are laughing at them. This is a fantastic illustration of this phenomenon. If you see a lot of other people running, there is a good chance that you will start running too, even if you don't know why. The instinct to congregate in groups is firmly engrained in animals since it has been so beneficial to their survival over the years. It is believed that the actions shown by a group or population as a whole represent the proper conduct. Even if it's not true, people tend to believe that having more people on your side gives you an advantage.

Therefore, whatever choice you make is either consciously or subconsciously influenced by what other individuals who have been in the same circumstances as you have done. The success of social proofing has been shown over and again by the entertainment industry, namely via the use of programs that include prerecorded laughing. The sound of people laughing that is played in some instances is referred to as "canned laughter." Even if they do not think what is being presented to be very humorous, the audience of the program will most likely join in on the artificial laughter that is being played. When members of such an audience are questioned about their impressions of the play at a later time, the majority of them will respond that it had many humorous moments. However, all that was done was a psychological trick in which they were placed in an environment in which everyone else was laughing, and as a result, they inferred that the most appropriate reaction was to laugh as well. This was done to make them believe that laughing was the most appropriate reaction.

Manipulators have the ability to employ social evidence as a method of persuasion in their work. They just need to persuade you that everyone else is engaging in the behavior in question. In the event that they want you to get into a contract with them despite the fact that it is not apparent to you, they may just show you the hundreds of other individuals who have signed the same deal. The fact that a lot of other individuals have previously signed the contract should provide you with some sense of reassurance and peace of mind. The social proofing strategy is most effective in settings where:

There is a lack of clarity; the target should not have any idea how to respond. It is very clear that they should not have been exposed to a circumstance comparable to the one from which they may draw conclusions. Because of this, the easiest approach for the target to make a choice is to think about what other people have done in the past and model their behavior after it.

There should be a consistent response from the rest of the group; the target's actions will be impacted by the behavior of the herd, not by the actions of individuals who are isolated within the group. As a result, the manipulator has the responsibility of ensuring that the other individuals involved in the same scenario come to the same conclusions. If the target observes any variations in the responses of other individuals, they will deviate from the behavior of the herd and make an effort to come up with their own choices.

These two requirements do not need any kind of physical production to exist. Conditions that are socially proofed may be generated in studios, as can be observed in programs with artificial laughter, which are mostly family-oriented television shows. The manipulator has the ability to build them verbally by informing the target that many other people are making the choice they anticipate you to make and that they have earned favorable benefits as a result of their decision. When this happens, the herd mentality kicks in, and people believe it is safer to behave in the same way as everyone else or make the same choice as others. The use of social evidence may be quite powerful, but only when the person being persuaded is uncertain or has never been in a similar circumstance before.

Chapter Forty-Eight

Framing

A mental frame is an individual's state of mind in regard to a particular subject or person. It is the lens that will judiciously gather and retain information with the purpose of directing a person toward a certain way of comprehending the world around them. When it comes to the practice of the art of persuasion, framing is a sort of reality manipulation in which the facts are manipulated on purpose. In order to accomplish one's goals in an appropriate manner, it is common practice to tell just part of the truth. This strategy has been around for centuries. For instance, politicians who are running for reelection are likely to embellish the accomplishments they have accomplished in the past. In the run-up to the election, people will evaluate the candidate based on their perception of whether or not they have a successful track record of providing services. It is also conceivable that the candidates representing the opposition would highlight the shortcomings made by those who were elected. Voters will be led to believe that everything is in turmoil as a result of this, and that a new leader is required as a result because the opposition candidate is the right match.

When employed in marketing, framing draws attention to products that have not been selling well, which increases the likelihood that such products will be purchased. A deft hand with the pricing structure is all that is required to pull off the con. For a limited amount of time, the sellers will raise the pricing of the goods, which will be seen by customers as a signal that there is a shortage of the things or that demand for them has grown. After then, the prices will be readjusted to the initial price, but they will note that they have been reduced by twenty percent. Buyers will look at the product with the perspective that it used to be costly but that the price has just been dropped, indicating that they should get it as soon as possible.

When social engineers successfully connect the reality of their targets with their expectations, framing has been successful. As a result, the approach only accomplishes half of the trick, while the target is responsible for finishing the trick in their own head. Framing may be accomplished in an effective manner in a variety of different methods. The following describe each of these:

1. Make statements that contribute to the formation of a certain context. If a manipulator wants you to think that he is a stockbroker, he will make statements that are consistent with what you anticipate brokers to say. For instance, he may take a call and consciously utter things out loud such as, "I'm sorry, I didn't hear you." "The stock X is now the most promising one for day trading, therefore my recommendation would be to avoid Y for the time being. Bearishness dominates the market at the moment. Regarding this matter, I will get back to you at a later time." They will have established a framework that is aligned with what you anticipate a stockbroker to know or say with just a simple phone call and the mention of stock brokerage terms. If the manipulator's true goal is to steal your money, the fact that you believe they are legitimate stockbrokers makes it much easier for them to pull off their plan.

2. Imply to a certain frame — If a manipulator is not very familiar with the expectations of a particular frame, they might simply imply to it in order to get over this limitation. They need just arrange the objectives in the form of a mental challenge. For instance, a manipulator selling counterfeit goods may simply ask a prospective victim, "do you realize how many people are crying to us to provide them with these products?" as a means of influencing their behavior. The targets will make it seem as if whatever is being offered is in very great demand, and that their discovery of the seller is a stroke of good luck.

3. Reiterate the framework, since it is a well-known adage that a falsehood that is repeated often enough will eventually be accepted as the truth. The same applies to the formulation of the question. If the manipulator is successful in feeding information into the frame, the target

will have no reason to question whether or not it is true. If the seller of counterfeit goods continues to receive many calls from "potential buyers" while having a conversation with the target, the target will be convinced that the item being sold to them is scarce, in high demand, and that they should purchase it as soon as possible in order to avoid missing out on the opportunity.

When the manipulator is equipped with strong presenting abilities, framing may be an extremely powerful tactic. After a frame has been implanted in a target's brain, it will obscure that person's judgment even more, which is exactly what the manipulator wants to happen.

Chapter Forty-Nine

Conclusion

In this chapter, we covered the many persuasive strategies that are currently in use and are shown to be successful. One example of this is the practice of reciprocation, in which a target is given a favor, and as a result of their feelings of obligation, they return an even greater favor. The second method is known as the obligation approach, and it involves a target being coerced into helping via moral, contractual, legal, or religious responsibilities. The third strategy was known as concession, and it included a manipulator agreeing to some conditions that were requested by a target but still imposing other conditions that solely benefited the manipulator. The fourth strategy was known as scarcity, in which manipulators would make some alternatives seem to be scarcer than they really were, primarily by applying time pressure. This leads a target to make hasty judgments because of the feeling of urgency, yet they end up committing themselves to transactions that are not in their best interests.

The fifth technique was called "commitment and consistency," and it consisted of a manipulator tricking a target into making a small commitment, which then only led to larger commitments that the target was required to honor in order to maintain consistency. This technique is known as "commitment and consistency." The sixth method was called "liking," and it consisted of providing the target with some kind of affirmation so that they would become captivated and more likely to deliver favors to the manipulator. The seventh strategy was known as social proof, and it encouraged targets to make particular judgments simply because others had made those same decisions. Last but not least, the chapter discussed framing, which is the process by which manipulators instill a certain mentality in their targets in order to make it simpler for themselves to exploit those targets. These strategies are fairly effective methods for convincing individuals to adhere to one's will or to comply with one's requests in order to achieve one's goals. They have been implemented in practice, just like the examples presented in the chapter have done. e shown.

Chapter Fifty

The human survival strategy that includes controlling other people is called social control. Even when they are very young, newborns have the ability to exert influence on their parents through wailing. They scream out for food when they are hungry, for love when they are lonely, to have their diapers changed when they have soiled them, and for a variety of other things as well. They are able to get what they want by only sobbing over it. Because it is evident that sobbing becomes fairly ineffectual as a technique of dominating other people later in life, one must acquire other methods that they may use to obtain what they want from other people in order to be successful.

Utilizing certain terms in a strategic manner is the most effective method. Words have the power to accomplish a lot of different things, such create, destroy, provide hope, stir up doubt, and generate dread. People may be hurt, healed, praised, confused, or humbled in a matter of seconds, all without any effort on their part physically. Your words have the potential to have a significant impact on the world around you. They bestow upon you the power to convince other people to fulfill your wants or to act in accordance with your demands. They may also bring about feelings of hopelessness and melancholy, as well as make you more susceptible to being influenced. Because words may cut both ways, one must exercise extreme caution while using them. Words are a powerful tool, and those who manipulate others are well aware of how they may use them to their advantage.

You may become resistant to manipulation and possess the ability to influence others rather than having them control you if you also find the power of your own words. However, this is only possible if you uncover the power that lies inside your own words. The purpose of this chapter is to teach you how to exert influence on others using the power of language. It is going to look at:

Fundamental aspects of efficient and successful communication Putting individuals in charge of their own choices by setting the stage

Chapter Fifty-One

Fundamental aspects of efficient and successful communication

There are a variety of careers in which one has to have a command of the art of wordplay in order to succeed. In the field of law enforcement, suspects are questioned in a certain manner so that authorities may corner them into admitting, confessing, or providing information to them. Even when dealing with recalcitrant respondents, journalists still need to be able to determine which phrases to employ to elicit answers from their sources. When working in fields such as these, it is necessary to have a fundamental understanding of certain ideas in order to make the most of the power contained inside one's own words. In the next part, we shall examine these fundamentals.

Listening

To ensure that the impression you want to achieve with your words is achieved, you must first be aware of the context in which you are speaking. Listening carefully is the most essential step in the process of turning your words into weapons. In order to correctly perceive various events or what other people are saying, you need to be an active listener.

The participants in many discussions fail to listen to one another because they are preoccupied with formulating what it is that they will say when it is finally their time to speak, which results in the argument devolving into a chaotic mess. It is necessary to be able to listen attentively and take in what other people have to say in order to appropriately plan how you will utilize your words to your benefit. Before you can answer, you must first understand the logic behind the positions taken by others.

One of the most frequent errors that individuals make is that they attempt to maintain control of a conversation by speaking more than they need to. In point of fact, all it takes to shift the discussion in a direction of your choosing is one well-planned statement. People are naturally gregarious, and you can glean a great deal about someone from the things that they tell about themselves. Even if you remain silent, they will react and continue to provide you with information that you may use to acquire control over them.

Having an appreciation for how other people see things

In order to communicate effectively with other people, it is necessary to comprehend the perspectives others hold on certain matters. Because you could say things out of ignorance if you don't comprehend the viewpoint of the audience, failing to understand their perspective might lead to problems. When you talk purely from your own point of view, you run the danger of an audience misinterpreting what you are saying. When you use other people's words to gain something from them, you need to communicate in a manner that corresponds to how they interpret the world or how they see it.

Creating a sense of uniqueness in other people

One often used proverb asserts that validation is the "quiet murderer of man." You have to make the person feel unique and important if you want to deepen your relationship with them or if you want them to offer you anything. They will feel at comfortable to share with you after they have been validated and have come to the realization that they matter. Before conducting interviews, members of the media will do their research to learn about any noteworthy accomplishments that the person being interviewed has to their name. The interviewer will begin by mentioning all of these accomplishments before proceeding with the interview in order to implement a strategic plan to make the interviewee feel unique. They will experience an increase in joy, leading to an increased willingness to communicate, even about topics that they would ordinarily keep private. If you are attempting to gain an edge via the use of your words, you will need as much information as you can get your hands on to confirm the claims of others. When someone gets validated, they will become cooperative and receptive to sharing information; as a result, you will have a greater chance of receiving what you want from them after they have achieved this status.

Being Self-aware

There is a power that your body emits that is not apparent to the naked eye, but is constantly felt by others around you. If you are able to enhance this force, you will have a better chance of gaining control of the other people. The way in which you portray yourself to people has an effect on the impression that they receive of you. The concept of self-awareness encompasses a wide variety of behaviors, including how you appear, move, smile, and greet other people, as well as the tone you use while speaking. The human brain has the capacity to interpret a great deal of information all at once. Even if you are delivering an outstanding speech, no one will trust what you have to say just because of the tone that you are using. You might even be badly dressed but talk in such a compelling manner that the audience would trust you despite your appearance.

As a result, it is essential for you to check that both your verbal and non-verbal modes of communication are effective in advancing your goals. It is important that your tone of voice, gestures, and facial expressions convey that you are the one in charge if you want other people to see you in that role. Some applicants rely on a certain strategy in order to maintain their self-assurance during the interview process. In order to take up as much physical space as possible, they sit in an upright position with their arms spread out and then talk in a low tone. They are thus perceived by the interviewers in an unconscious manner as having a high level of confidence.

When you are walking down the street, there is another strategy you may use to prevent embarrassing collisions with other people. This strategy involves both of you unwittingly shifting from left to right in order to avoid running into each other again. You just need to keep your head up and keep looking in the direction of your target. When you stare at individuals directly in the eyes, you increase the likelihood that they may walk into you. However, if you keep your gaze fixed on the distance ahead of you, they will point the route out to you. People will anticipate your route and move out of it in order to avoid colliding with you if they notice that you are traveling with your attention fixed on a location farther in the distance than they are. In a similar vein, it is important to have a healthy sense of self-awareness in order to exercise control over the image that you give to other people. The people who listen to you speak need to acquire the impression that you are self-assured and have a destination in mind. Therefore, it is not hard for them to think that what you are saying is both intentional and accurate.

While you communicate, other people are formulating an idea of who you are based on these fundamental concepts. If you desire something from other people, the way in which they define you will impact your chances of being successful in gaining that object from them. You may exert influence on other people if you show yourself as someone who matters, who is in power, and who can be trusted.

Chapter Fifty-Two

Putting individuals in charge of their own choices by setting the stage

When attempting to exert influence on other people, the words you choose to use are important. You may use certain phrases to catch people's attention and even have them eager to offer you all you need from them if you utilize such words correctly. People tend to place themselves into one of two groups in the majority of social settings: leaders and followers. You have to choose the right phrases in order to catapult yourself to the front of the pack. Words that express one's status as a leader or a person in authority are used by parents, teachers, managers, religious leaders, and politicians, among others. The actions and cognitive patterns of others are altered as a direct result of hearing these remarks.

If a teacher cautions a student not to make a certain error again, the student will probably refrain from doing that error in the future, even if they are unaware of the potential consequences of doing so. In a similar vein, politicians will encourage people to vote for them or to support their political goals, and the majority of people will comply with these requests. They are not going to challenge these orders since they were given by a person in a position of power. The same dynamics may be seen in a group conversation. If you are participating in a group chat and then employ authoritative language, the other people participating in the conversation will do anything you tell them to do without questioning it. People will follow people who demonstrate that they are in a position of power. Your objective should be to first put yourself in a position of power and then exert your will on the people around you.

Priming is the technique that will most effectively bring about these two outcomes. At this point, you will provide your targets with something that will have an effect on the behaviors or choices they do in the future. Priming is an unconscious process, and as a result, the people you are targeting are never made aware of the eventual game that you are playing. The subconscious has a significant impact on humans' ability to make choices, despite the fact that people feel their decisions are free and theirs alone to choose. Consequently, everything that is implanted in a person's subconscious will have a part in how their conscious mind processes ideas and makes decisions. This provides you the opportunity to influence them to behave in the manner you desire, or to make them feel more inclined to give you what you want. A few instances of how you can "prime" individuals to boost their attentiveness and then manipulate them are shown below:

i. Instilling an innate sense of individualism in people — If you want people to support a certain cause or feel motivated to overcome obstacles, you need to instill an innate sense of individualism in them. You may increase their feeling of who they are by using terms like "I," "solely," "different," and "own" in the sentences you construct for them. Because of this, they will be less inclined to adhere to past opinions that were pushed to them by others, and they will be more willing to embrace any individualistic notions that you have.

ii. Priming others to be collaborative - if you need assistance with a task or want people to work together, you may prime them to be collaborative before you ask for assistance or instruct them to perform something as a team. This is especially useful if you want people to join hands with you. You may choose to use phrases and words into your sentences such as "work as a team," "stronger together," "us," "we shall," and "our." As soon as they hear numerous of these statements, their subconscious begins to alter how inclined they are to join in group activities or assist out with work.

iii. Inspiring individuals to have strong moral convictions by requiring them to publicly swear an oath of office before assuming public office is one method of achieving this goal. Oaths are used in the legal system to ensure that witnesses are truthful in their testimony. When you speak to individuals with the intention of coercing them into confessing or admitting to doing something, you have the opportunity to prime their moral identities. You may start with quotations from various religions or statements from persons who are known to have been very forthright. In spite of the fact that, on the surface level, individuals may not feel the effect, their subconscious is inclined toward a certain moral identity, and this will influence the choices that they make and the way that they behave.

After you have primed individuals, you can then make your request, and since you have already planted the notion in their subconscious, it is probable that they will reply precisely way you intended them to because of the thought you planted.

Chapter Fifty-Three

Conclusion

Words are strong weapons that can be used to accomplish any desired consequence in other people. You only need to know how to utilize them properly. You may exert influence on other people by using them almost often. You start displaying signs of being able to exert control over other people from a very young age, since it is a human survival strategy to do so. As you become older, using your words becomes your primary method of exerting influence over other people and gaining what you want from them. Words have the power to create specific sensations in others as well as influence them to form an opinion about how you present yourself. Exploiting words, on the other hand, does not imply talking more than other people; rather, it is all about being economical with the words you use and using them in a way that is sensible. Certain guiding principles are required to be adhered to in order to exert influence on other people. These principles may be taught from professions that depend heavily on the power of words. If you want to understand more about your audience or your objectives, you need to become an active listener. You must therefore make an effort to see things from their point of view in order to prevent getting into unneeded disputes that are the result of misconceptions.

You need to find a way to make your audience feel that they are likewise unique and valued. Last but not least, anytime you approach other people and have a conversation with them, you need to ensure that you are self-aware. These principles help people form accurate impressions of you, which in turn allows you more leeway in determining how they do so. You may begin to exert influence over them by employing certain phrases that are able to go very deep into the subconscious minds they are operating from. Priming is the process of exposing individuals to certain items in order to influence their later decision making. Priming occurs when you expose someone to particular things. You may condition individuals to behave in a variety of desirable ways, including cooperating, being individualistic, being morally upright, and many other behaviors. After priming them, you will have power over their ability to make decisions, and it will be simple for you to get what you want from them. them.

In dark According to psychological research, those who prey on others often search for certain vulnerability signs in order to select the perfect victim. Every single human being has specific traits that, when combined, might render them more susceptible to harm. On the other hand, these features are shaped in part by the environment in which a person is raised as a component of the process of being nurtured. Because of this, the success rates of a manipulator change depending on the level of nurturing provided to the target. Respect for authority, the desire to avoid conflict, a guilty conscience, and a sense of moral obligation to provide a hand are some of the basic human characteristics that may be used to an advantage by manipulators.

These characteristics help define a person's personality to varied degrees. People are often institutionalized since the policies of many social setups are based on these characteristics. Some individuals eventually lose these characteristics when they are subjected to varying surroundings or experiences over their lifetime. For instance, a psychopath loses the feeling that they have a responsibility to assist other people. However, these characteristics are never eliminated entirely, and with the appropriate words or circumstances, they may still be used to one's advantage.

Even the most hardest criminal will care for his family, just as those who engage in humanitarian help would care for those who have been affected by a calamity. In spite of the fact that the criminal is planning to commit heinous crimes against other people, they nevertheless retain some of the qualities that are characteristic of those who engage in the field of humanitarian help. As a result, manipulators have a working ground at their disposal, which gives them the capacity to utilize it to abuse anybody. Therefore, there is no one who is immune to being sensitive, but some people are more susceptible than others. To begin abusing various individuals, manipulators merely need to have a basic understanding of which strings to pull in each individual. Several indicators of susceptibility are looked for in order to establish which targets may be readily influenced. This chapter will explain the indicators that reveal the vulnerabilities of people to their predators and will provide advice on how individuals might avoid being manipulated.

Chapter Fifty-Four

Indicators of susceptibility

Naivety

Naiveté is an excellent vulnerability signal that might indicate a target will be an easy victim. People who are naive often give the impression of having a poor grasp of the actual world. They do not base their decisions on their impressions but rather on the ideas that guide them in life. For instance, they can wrongly believe that the people who are taking advantage of them are merely well-meaning friends or family members who are always in need of assistance, rather than seeing that they are just being used for their own benefit. Empathy and the sense that one is compelled to assist other people both play a role in the development of naiveté. By making early steps to test the degrees of trust or patience their targets have with relatively new individuals, manipulators may determine whether or not the people they are trying to take advantage of are naive.

People who are truthful

It's common knowledge that toddlers have a refreshingly straightforward honesty. On the other hand, as adolescents become older, they realize that it is better to keep certain things to themselves and not discuss them with just anyone. However, since this is a consequence of how a person is raised, not everyone has the opportunity to gain this knowledge. Because of this, there are certain people who continue throughout their life to be excessively forthright. Persons who are willing to exclusively disclose the truth about their choices, suspicions, mental processes, personal lives, and so on are easy prey for people who are skilled at manipulating others. Finding a target who is willing to act like an open book is a lucky discovery for a manipulator.

People who are materialistic

One of the things that drives people is the desire to accumulate more resources. They get up and go to work in order to accumulate adequate riches so that they may live lifestyles that are more pleasant for them. With the other hand, some individuals develop a fixation on the concept of accumulating as much assets as they can, to the point where they become materialistic. This need for more may be used by manipulators to lure their prey into dubious business arrangements. In most cases, the targets are offered misleading claims that they would make extraordinary financial benefits. People who place a high value on worldly possessions will ultimately give in to their greed, and they will be willing to give up what the manipulators have asked them to give up in order to increase their own fortune.

Elderliness

The world is a terrible place, and becoming older increases one's risk of being taken advantage of. The elderly are a common target for con artists since they are seen to be easier to fool than younger people. The elderly are unable to multitask owing to both their advanced age and the physical restrictions that come with it. If people are bombarded with a lot of information that seems to have come from a reliable source, they will trust the one who provided it. A scam on them is also less likely to be discovered by them. Because of this, individuals are able to rapidly part with their money by providing it to others who claim to double it, give them and their family a profitable vacation, and provide many other benefits.

The need to have one's needs met.

The ability to successfully say "no" is a struggle that most individuals must encounter. If one wants to make other people happy or if one wants to be accepted, validated, and to be in a good relationship, the best course of action seems to be to agree to their wishes. It was previously remarked by Tony Blair that the foundation of leadership is not saying yes but rather no. He went on to suggest that it was often fairly simple to answer in the affirmative. The desire to make other people happy is a characteristic that is universal to all people. They typically do not want to become involved in any kind of disagreement at any time. They also make an effort to avoid disappointing or offending other people. They would rather be inconvenienced in order to avoid the possibility of saying no and causing harm to others. As a result, they end up agreeing to whatever it is that they are requested to do. If the manipulator discovers that the target has a strong need to be pleased, they are in a prime position to take advantage of this trait by making demands that indicate they would suffer distress in the event that their wishes are not fulfilled. For instance, a person may pretend that they are stranded in a distant town and are completely out of money in order to make a case for receiving financial assistance. Even if they are strapped with cash, the target will almost certainly go out of their way to locate something that they can send.

a lack of dependence on oneself

There are certain individuals who are unable to depend on their capacity to carry out tasks by themselves. Therefore, even while making judgments on little matters, they need the backing of other people. People who lack self-reliance often have the habit of seeking the opinion of others before making almost every major life decision. For instance, they will not sign up for a gym membership without first determining from another person whether or not it is worthwhile. They will also not buy certain things unless they have received confirmation from another individual that doing so would be beneficial. People who have difficulty relying on themselves will make easy prey for others who want to manipulate them. They will simply need to form relationships with these types of individuals or get closer to them and demonstrate their extensive knowledge on a variety of subjects. As a consequence of this, the targets will increasingly begin to depend on them. The manipulators are now in a position to take advantage of their newly acquired power and feast on the targets.

People who have difficulty relying on themselves often develop an emotional dependence on the people around them. Therefore, their contentment originates from the joy experienced by other individuals. Their emotions are dependent on the actions of others. Individuals who are emotionally reliant almost often struggle with feelings of isolation, which is a normal experience for people who are adjusting to new environments. For instance, a new worker who feels isolated and alone on the inside may exhibit indications of emotional reliance on their first day of work. This is because they are exposed to a new environment. A manipulator might take advantage of a situation by offering the target company, and over time, the target will grow emotionally reliant on the manipulator. Following a period of a few months, the manipulator will be able to begin leeching off of the victim. The victim will not complain, even though it is obvious that they are being used, since they are emotionally reliant on the manipulator and do not want to upset them. Additionally, the victim does not want to hurt the manipulator.

People with a Pollyannish accent

As was discussed in a prior chapter, it has been noted that certain people who have been abused would always return to individuals who assaulted them. This is something that has been seen. It has been reported that former citizens of oppressive regimes, such as the one in North Korea, are making their way back into the nation despite being well aware of the dangers that lie in store for them there. The trouble with people is that they always strive to find a reasonable explanation for everything that occurs to them. In the end, they figure out a method to put everything back in order. They will even find ways to rationalize why others had to be harmful to them and would use those justifications to justify their behavior. Interactions in which targets strive to rationalize why they have been misled and blame themselves for such relationships are fertile ground for the development of manipulative tendencies.

The Pollyannish individuals will also have an overly optimistic sensation that everything will go as planned, thus it is important to avoid focusing on the negative aspects of the situation. As a result, they never fail to extend the benefit of the doubt to others around them. People who always look on the bright side of situations make it simple for manipulators to take advantage of them. They may not even be aware that they are being taken advantage of. When questioned on certain topics, the manipulator should just have plausible answers ready to provide. For instance, a manipulator may take some money out of a target's bank account, and when this is found, the manipulator could claim that there was an urgent need for money from the target's family, and that the money will be reimbursed. The victim will most likely not pursue the matter further and will instead conclude that there must have been sufficient justifications for the money being moved without their permission.

Lack of ability to be aggressive

The capacity to freely communicate one's thoughts, emotions, and requirements is what we mean when we talk about assertiveness. On the other hand, there are those individuals who choose not to voice either their sentiments or their thoughts. In the past, there existed a stereotype that was generally accepted by society, which said that women were connected with passive activities. Although this stereotypical belief that women should behave submissively when in the company of males is still prevalent in certain nations, it seems to have been mostly eradicated in the majority of the rest of the globe. A manipulator is able to take full advantage of a target when the target is non-assertive since it provides the right setting for them to do so.

Even while it is frequently the product of preconceptions, insecurity and lack of assertiveness may also be the result of poor self-esteem and a lack of self-worth. The manipulators will take advantage of such sentiments by making choices that the targets won't challenge because they know they won't. These choices will almost always end up helping the manipulator and hurting the person who is being manipulated. A manipulative manager, for instance, may inform their staff that rather than putting in the standard 40 hours of labor per week, they would now be required to put in the standard 48 hours. Regardless of the provisions laid forth in the employment contract, the workers will not file any formal complaints if they lack the confidence to stand up for themselves. The passiveness will work to the favor of the manipulator, who will benefit from the victim's continued timidity and the victim's inability to voice their thoughts.

Making it difficult for others to use their power over you

The signals mentioned above are only some of the many tools that manipulators have at their disposal. Naturally, you will have some of the characteristics of personality that are actively being utilized by those who want to manipulate you. The fact that they have been manipulated is something that dawns on a great number of individuals much too late in the game. As a result, it is of the highest significance that you learn how to transform yourself from an easy target for manipulators into one that is difficult and cannot be taken advantage of in an easy manner. You must have a fundamental comprehension of the following aspects of manipulation:

Anyone and everything is capable of manipulating another person, and the odds are high that you will be influenced by individuals who you consider to be your family or friends. People who manipulate others have little respect for the limits of relationships. Because of this, you should always have in the back of your mind the possibility that anybody may influence you if they so want. If you discover that you have been manipulated, you will very certainly have feelings of betrayal, of having been taken advantage of, and of being helpless. No matter what kind of relationship you have with the manipulator, they will not feel much of anything since they are just driven by their own egotistical goals. This is true regardless of the nature of your connection to them. Be wary of random acts of concern, love, or politeness from strangers since they are often unwelcome and unwarranted in social situations. Many forms of manipulation start with a period known as the honeymoon phase, which is designed to make you relax and trust the manipulator.

You have the power to put an end to manipulation. While you may not be able to alter the person who is influencing you, you always have the option to modify your personality so that you are resistant to being manipulated. You won't be able to put an end to the manipulation unless you avoid walking into the traps that the manipulators have placed for you. You have to accept responsibility for the choices you make and refuse to give anybody the power to manipulate you into making poor choices. You won't regain control of the situation unless you decide to cease behaving in a way that the manipulator wants you to. It is not worth your time to pursue a romantic connection if maintaining it requires you to constantly appease the other person.

The practice of manipulation expands - those who manipulate you will often look for new methods that they may use to take total control of you. They must, however, proceed with extreme caution in order to avoid generating suspicion, which might impede their ability to achieve long-term success. As a result, you will most likely become aware of the manipulation that is taking place. It might take the shape of reliance on the manipulator or helplessness in the face of that person. The more you give in to the manipulator's demands, the more vulnerable you become to their influence. Therefore, you should attempt to end the cycle of manipulation as soon as possible.

To briefly restate the arguments made above, anybody has the potential to manipulate others, manipulation can be stopped, and the problem will only become worse if it is not stopped. The most effective strategy to protect yourself from being exploited is to first provide indications to those who are trying to manipulate you that you are a difficult target and then to resist giving in to any of their manipulation techniques. The following are some strategies that licensed psychologists have suggested as effective ways to protect oneself from falling victim to manipulators:

Take your time - manipulators need to exploit a sense of urgency in order to create a situation in which you are required to make significant choices without taking the time to carefully consider the many alternatives that are accessible to you. This is how individuals find themselves in precarious romantic relationships, poisonous jobs, pyramid scams, and other similar situations. When faced with making crucial choices, you should always take your time. You must also make it very apparent that you are not reliant on the permission of the manipulator in order to take your time to deliberate over your options or to decide not to make any decision at all.

Do not attempt to defend your choices; instead, provide obvious and uncomplicated responses to those who attempt to manipulate you. If you are pressured into joining an investment club that seems to be a pyramid scam, you should simply refuse to participate and should not provide an explanation for your decision. When you rationalize a choice, you offer others who are trying to manipulate you an opportunity to attempt to persuade you even more. Therefore, you should not attempt to explain yourself or engage in a follow-up conversation. This will deter the manipulator from attempting to attack you again in the future.

Allow yourself to experience unpleasant sensations. Manipulators often exploit uncomfortable sentiments such as fear and guilt to gain control over their victims. On the other hand, you need to have the capacity to tolerate the possibility of being exposed to shame or anxiety. If a manipulator attempts to trick you into falling into a guilt trap, all you need to do is learn to live with the guilt for the time being, but resist giving in to their demands. They will cease targeting you if they understand that you have a thick skin and that their attempts to make you to feel guilty are unsuccessful.

Expose the manipulation - as long as there is harmony between you and the manipulator, the manipulation will continue as long as you don't call it out for what it is. Because of this, you need to produce a disturbance in the connection and point out any manipulative demands or tendencies the other person may have. The manipulator realizes that you are onto him since you have done this, which confirms his suspicions.

You need to tell the person who is manipulating you that you have already identified their final aims and have recognized that the manipulation strategy that is being used against you will be futile. This will cause the manipulator to stop manipulating you. Keep in mind that you should not attempt to defend these remarks so that they cannot affect the narrative in any way.

Establish your own conditions; if you are already involved in any kind of connection with a manipulator, you need to do this as soon as possible in order to protect yourself. For instance, you may warn a relative who has the ability to manipulate you that you would not be able to do anything special for them and that this applies to all favors.

You will have established a barrier that will reduce the manipulator's drive and enthusiasm.

Be prepared to make concessions after being the victim of manipulation. If you discover that you may have been the target of manipulation, you should be prepared to shift the power dynamic in your favor. You should be willing to modify any commitments or agreements you have made with someone who has previously been shown to be manipulative. You may easily explain to them that the circumstances have changed, and that as a result, you are unable to carry out what you had previously committed to doing.

Chapter Fifty-Five

Conclusion

In this chapter, we have explored the essence of manipulation and spoken about the indications that manipulators use to identify easy targets. It has been shown that there are some human characteristics that are shared by all people and that may be used by manipulators. As a result of the fact that they are present in various people to differing degrees, manipulators often need to identify those individuals who may be readily used in order to achieve their goals. The characteristics of innocence, honesty, materialism, elderliness, desire to please, poor self-reliance, optimism, and lack of assertiveness have been identified as indicators of vulnerability and have been addressed. The manipulators will engage in conversation with a variety of persons to determine whether or not these individuals display the signals. Those individuals who exhibit these tells are considered to be easy targets. Following that, the chapter has shown that it is feasible to make oneself a challenging target for those who engage in manipulative behavior. It outlines a number of strategies that may be used in order to put up a fight against manipulators and manipulative tendencies. These strategies effectively counteract the effects of manipulative techniques. and drive manipulators away.

Chapter Fifty-Six

Case Studies

Leonardo Leonardo da Vinci once remarked that the only time you really belong to yourself is when you are by yourself. He continued by saying that if you are in the company of another person, you only possess fifty percent of yourself. When considered in the context of humans preying on one another, the meaning of this remark is that you are more likely to be exploited if you are accompanied by other people. Therefore, your only real defense against being taken advantage of is likely to be your ability to isolate yourself. You should now have a better understanding of why and how people prey on one another thanks to the discussion of the finer points of dark psychology in the chapters that came before this one. The conversation that will take place in this chapter will present real-life examples of people exploiting one another. Because there are so many different ways in which manipulation might take place, it is impossible for this chapter to address them all. On the other hand, there will be several instances that fall into either of the two types of manipulation, namely covert manipulation and overt manipulation.

Chapter Fifty-Seven

Covert manipulation examples

These sorts of predators are sneaky because they first give the impression that they are likable individuals who exude a lot of charm. After someone has earned your confidence, they will gradually start to reveal who they really are. They might not constantly maintain an outgoing demeanor, which may give the impression that they are introverted. In spite of this, they are self-centered and boastful, and they have a contemptuous attitude toward the people around them. Because their goal is to play the "nice person" card in all of their interactions with targets until it is the appropriate moment to start exploiting them, these will be used largely in the first contacts they have with their targets. The examples that follow are some real-world applications of this kind of manipulation.

Anna

Because she portrayed herself as a humanitarian to the victim, the two of them became very close to one another and became his buddy. She often spoke about the humanitarian causes in which she was actively involved as well as the non-profit organizations, such as UN agencies, with which she was working. Her victim was unaware that Anna's purpose in all of this discussion was just to give her a positive character. Anna did not, in her heart of hearts, care about anybody. The victim details how Anna approached whatever relation-ship she formed with an attitude of superiority and exploitation of her victim. She always had the attitude that she deserved favors but never did anything to earn them back.

The victim eventually came to the conclusion that Anna treated the majority of her friends with contempt. It seemed as if these friends were less capable and were not deserving of her company. Her attitude, tone of voice, and body language all indicated that this was what she was thinking, even if she did not directly state it. After she got intoxicated and said that all she wanted in life was for others to adore or worship her, her buddy began to pull away from her and become less emotionally invested in their relationship.

Simply because Anna want to be the center of attention, she was skilled at dismissing the sentiments of others and responding negatively to what others had to say. Anna was under the impression that the spotlight would shift away from her if one of her close friends articulated an insightful notion or expressed thoughts in a way that elicited powerful responses. As a result, she was forced to engage in deceptive behavior in order to maintain everyone's focus on her. On the other hand, she presented herself to the general public in a way that was kind and full of compassion.

Tom

Tom was an entrepreneur who was also well regarded as a cornerstone of the town in which he resided. This respect stemmed from the fact that Tom lived there. In the company of other individuals at various occasions, he often engaged in philosophical and ethical discourse. He preferred to use himself as an example by stating that he was guided by strong moral convictions, labored extremely hard to become self-sufficient, and accepted responsibility for directing the community. He said that he worked very hard to become self-sufficient. Any discussion he had with other people revolved around the topic of personal values, and he presented himself to others as the one who best exemplified morality. On the other hand, a more in-depth examination of his family might demonstrate the opposite. Tom was not present in any aspect of their lives. He does not like spending time with his wife or children as much as he enjoys spending time with "the community." He would explain his reasoning for this by stating that his children needed to learn how to fend for themselves and that when he was the same age, his own father was not very involved in his life.

Tom would often remark about how difficult his upbringing was, particularly the times when his children would beg for money and he would do whatever he could to avoid giving it to them.

When his own children asked him to be a father for even a little moment, he was always prepared with the perfect response to put an end to their pleading.

Outside of the confines of his family, he became notorious for breaking the commitments that he had made. In the event that he was challenged, he would simply disregard anybody who approached him. For instance, he might assure a family that he would provide a specific financial amount, but he would never follow through with his word. If you asked him why, he would just avoid answering the question. When he broke his vows, he felt that his character was beyond reproach and that no one should confront him about it. Because he believed himself to be better than other people, he resented the fact that other people sought to challenge him. This caused him to see others with such contempt. This was what differentiated him from other individuals in the world.

A typical person would apologize when they were wrong, do their best to show empathy (particularly toward their own children), and present an explanation when they broke a commitment they made. Tom was a hypocrite who was only concerned in giving the impression to other people that he was a compassionate individual deserving of the title "pillar of the community" because he believed that this would be beneficial to his company. He aspired to be seen as the utmost embodiment of high moral and ethical standards at all times. He was unwilling to accept responsibility for anything at any time. Since of this, he was able to achieve financial success and a prominent place in the society; nevertheless, his family had a difficult time of it in general because he sought to control every area of their life.

The youngsters had no intention of ever owning toys or participating in the activities that their contemporaries were participating in. In addition to this, he was beyond criticism to the point that no one in the whole community would dare to rebuke him.

A mother who is secretly a narcissist.

In this particular instance, the victims were the young members of a family that had serious problems. They did not get to enjoy their childhood and their mother used them as emotional trash cans instead of treating them with respect. At first, they believed that they had no choice but to remain in a household in which the father was the abuser and would subject them to emotional, verbal, and physical mistreatment. On the other hand, they quickly recognized that their mother was not much improved. The mother often vented her frustrations on her children, but she paid little attention to the challenges they faced in their own lives. The mother would vent her frustrations on her daughter on occasion in this manner. On the other hand, when the daughter had issues of her own, her mother did not want to provide any aid.

The mother did nothing to stop the overtly narcissistic father from abusing her children despite the fact that she was there for many years of the abuse. At times, she would cast the children in the role of the victim and even take the side of the child's violent father. Nevertheless, when the father started abusing her as well, she would weep in front of her children, and it was their responsibility to console and soothe her. In this situation, the children were put in the position of acting as their own parents, which was analogous to the concept of "reverse parenting." Whenever the mother was subjected to verbal or physical abuse at the hands of the father, she would make it seem as though it was the responsibility of the kid to care for her in the role of a mother. In spite of the fact that the mother did not intervene to protect the children when they were subjected to verbal or physical abuse at the hands of the father, she exploited the children's emotional resources to her advantage when she was the one who was being assaulted. Because of this, the children were raised in an unstable home where they were unable to depend on either of their parents.

People who engage in covert manipulation like being the focus of attention. They are despotic and dictatorial in a more covert manner. They will also continue to reassure everyone around them that they are excellent individuals who possess attributes worthy of respect. This is the strategy that they use most often in order to increase the number of people who like them shortly before they begin to prey on those individuals. Those who are close to a covert narcissist, such as friends or family, are the only people who are aware of their behavior. They are going to keep this secret from everyone else. However, they often make public statements about how empathetic, charitable, or trustworthy they are; as a result, you may use all of these characteristics as warning signs that they are attempting to manipulate you. People who are really decent are not the kind to go about bragging about how wonderful they are; rather, their deeds speak for themselves.

Those who engage in covert manipulation often utter nasty things in a nonchalant manner. Because of cognitive dissonance, it takes victims a significant amount of time to come to the realization that these individuals are not who they say they are. When an individual does kind acts in public but cruel acts behind closed doors, it might be difficult for a victim to understand how to interpret the cruel activities. They will go so far as to attempt to comprehend the motivations behind the individual's actions. However, after a considerable amount of time spent observing the narcissist, it will become abundantly evident that he or she has two personas: one is intended for the scrutiny of the public, while the other is reserved for private interactions.

Chapter Fifty-Eight

Manipulation in plain sight

When someone engages in overt manipulation, they do not attempt to conceal the fact that they are exploiting other people. Those who engage in overt manipulation have an inflated and fictitious sense of their own superiority, which leads them to see others as beneath them. An overt narcissist will have an excessive sense of their own self-importance, intelligence, superiority, and competitiveness. They will also have an inflated ego. Because of this, they develop a desire to control, exploit, and devalue others, as well as a condescending attitude toward those around them. They often exhibit feelings such as enthusiasm, boredom, rage, and envy in social situations. They have temperaments that are difficult to anticipate, they adopt a straightforward approach to achieving their goals, and they engage in behaviors that are rash, dangerous, and careless. They have a high level of competitiveness, an aggressive nature, and the desire to move up any hierarchy as quickly as possible. The following are case studies of overt narcissists, the majority of whom had positions of power in their own societies.

Idi Amin

Idi Amin is considered by many to be one of the most heinous dictators and the worst that the world has seen in the previous one hundred years. This portrayal can be seen in a number of movies. In 1971, he orchestrated an overthrow of the democratically elected president of Uganda, which marked the beginning of an eight-year government in the nation that was responsible for the deaths of more than 300,000 people and the expulsion of many foreign businesspeople. Amin, much like other grandiose narcissists, had an exaggerated sense of how important he was to the world, and as a result, he craved adoration from everyone. In 1971, when he assumed control of the government, he released political prisoners and made a pledge that he would turn power over to the people. This was his first public display of the bad side of his personality. Because of this, the majority of Ugandans adore and support him.

On the other hand, he quickly started his rant in which he massacred individuals and then demanded that other people show him adoration. Additionally, he wanted to keep the allegiance of his men, and as a reward for their service, he decided to give them the stores whose Asian proprietors he had forced to leave the nation. Idi Amin had a bloated ego, and some of the films from the time period that are still accessible show him boasting to interviewers that Ugandans like him and that he is highly brilliant.

Amin, much like any other overt narcissist, put others' worth below his own. He would give orders for the murder of individuals and their families whom he did not like and who he felt threatened him. Even the murder of his own wife was one of his orders. Idi Amin was characterised by a number of characteristics, one of which was the fact that he did not tolerate criticism in any form. He used terror to control people and secret police to murder anybody he suspected of criticizing him. He used fear to control people and kill anyone he suspected of criticizing him. When he heard a report that a talking tortoise had foretold his demise, he became highly worried. As a result, he changed his guards and rescheduled his vacation plans as a result of his concerns.

Amin lacks the capacity for empathy, to conclude. Amin made the decision to remain in power despite the fact that he was aware that, as a result of the expulsion of foreign businesspeople, he was destroying the economy of the nation. However, his rule was short-lived because of a botched raid against a neighboring country, during which his army was soundly crushed, and rebels quickly regained control of the nation.

A Bully

At a facility that provided therapy for adolescents, a new character coach by the name of Dr. George Simon saw a young man constantly flicking the ears of a child who sat in front of him. It was obvious that the youngster was upset by this, as shown by the fact that he sometimes turned around to demand that the bully cease his behavior. However, he continued as if nothing had happened despite the fact that it was obvious that his behaviors were making others feel uncomfortable. When Dr. Simon reported this to the administration of the institution, he was informed that the bully just had some underlying anger problems or was sad, and as a result, he was adversely channeling his frustrations. In other words, the bully was acting out his frustrations by bullying others.

Dr. Simon made the decision to address the young man and inquire as to the motivation behind his bullying behavior against other people. The bully only said that it was enjoyable to act in such a manner. As a result, he engaged in all of this behavior just for the excitement of it and had no regard for the repercussions that his actions had on the lives of other people. Dr. Simon claims that the incident provided him with the most valuable education he has ever received about predatory aggressors. They are psychopathic and have no consideration for the welfare of others. Because of this, they will prioritize their own gratification above that of others. This scenario may explain a number of different instances of bullying encounters, including those in which individuals give their sympathies to both the victim and the aggressor on the basis that they believe there are deeper problems that are driving the bullying conduct. On the other hand, there are numerous instances in which the bully is only a predatory aggressor and is not attempting to cope with a painful past but rather is having fun at the cost of other people.

Robert Pickton

It is believed that he murdered more than 50 individuals in cold blood, the most of them were sex workers from the city of Vancouver. He was a farmer from the province of British Columbia. It is reported that Robert would drive around Vancouver on occasion and invite people who worked in the commercial sex industry into his vehicle. After that, he would make a deal with them, promising money and narcotics in exchange for their companionship on the journey back to his property. The majority of the victims, under the belief that they would get paid far more, would immediately comply with Pickton's requests and join him. On the other hand, it is reported that he savagely killed them on his farm and mutilated their remains after the fact. After that, he would give them to his pigs to eat. Investigators discovered evidence that Pickton was also selling human remains with pig parts such as intestines to a business that processed items such as shampoo and detergent. This information was uncovered as a result of the investigation that was conducted.

When asked to explain how they dealt with the complaints of so many missing women who were later discovered to have been killed by Pickton, the Vancouver Police Department was at a loss for words. In addition, there were claims that some of the victims were able to flee from Pickton's property, despite the fact that police officers had been alerted that Pickton had kidnapped and stabbed them. The police officers, however, did nothing to help the victims. After such revelations from his victims, it is suspected that Pickton's financial standing may have played a factor in keeping him out of prison. However, the testimony of a farm worker was sufficient to start inquiries into Pickton's activities, which ultimately led to his arrest, prosecution, and punishment for the crimes he committed.

Chapter Fifty-Nine

Russel Williams

There are eerie rumors circulating about a former Colonel in the Canadian Armed Forces who was a serial killer and murderer in the past. In 2010, he received many punishments, including two life sentences and numerous other terms. Williams admitted to committing burglaries, sexual assaults, and first-degree murders, among other crimes. In the courtroom, he entered a guilty plea to all 88 of the accusations that were being brought against him. Even though he expressed remorse when he pleaded guilty, many people were taken aback by the severity of his offenses since they were unprecedented in Ontario. At first, Russell's antisocial activity consisted of relatively minor break-ins during which he would just take the victims' underwear without causing them any further damage. After that, he moved on to more serious crimes, such as sexual assault and murder, in which he would break into the houses of his victims, rape them, and then kill them. A strange conclusion might be drawn from the fact that he would steal their undergarments, snap pictures of their dead bodies, and engage in sexual activity on their beds. In addition to this, it is reported that he followed up with the police reports for each of the crimes he committed and kept some of the documents he was given.

In one incident, Williams used his position as a base station to obtain entry into the home of a female corporal, where he brutally assaulted and ultimately killed her. He documented the whole event by taking photographs. After that, he went on to take her undergarments, which by this point had become somewhat of a hallmark act for him. His most recent assault was committed on a lady, whom he abducted, then brought to his cabin, where he tormented her for a whole day before finally murdering her and disposing of her corpse. In addition to taking images, he also captured a four-hour video clip of the contact that he had with the person. It was because of this act that he was apprehended, as law enforcement investigators began searching for specific tire tracks that had been left close to the residence of the victim.

Williams was apprehended by the cops after the tire tracks of the Pathfinder he was driving matched those of the tracks left by the vehicle. He was hauled in for interrogation, during which he immediately began admitting to the atrocities he had committed. After his punishment, the Canadian Forces were so embarrassed by his behavior that they tore his uniform and decorations to shreds as a sign of their disgust. Additionally, his Pathfinder was decimated and smashed to pieces. In spite of a request from the prosecution that the video clips and photographs that Williams took be disposed of, the judge ruled that these items must be retained since it is possible that they may be relevant at Williams' parole hearing.

As can be seen from the previous examples, blatant narcissists present a significant risk to other people. One trend that may be seen is that the vast majority of openly narcissistic people thrive in authoritative roles. Idi Amin was a guy who proclaimed himself to be the president of Uganda, Pickton was a wealthy businessman, and Williams was a military colonel. Although holding these powerful positions may have allowed them to avoid the repercussions of their conduct for a while, in the end, justice will catch up with those responsible.

Chapter Sixty

Conclusion

Case studies from both covert and overt forms of manipulation, which are the two types of manipulation discussed in this chapter, have been examined. The first three case studies presented here were successful in capturing real-life examples of covert manipulation. As can be seen, the first step in covert manipulation is often for the offenders to put on masks in order to give the impression that they are decent people to the target audience. As soon as they have gained the confidence of their victims, they come clean about their ulterior motives and begin to take advantage of them. The three examples given here—Anna, Tom, and the covert narcissist mother—illustrate that covert manipulators want to take the spotlight whenever possible. They are also interested in maintaining a positive public image. Only those individuals who are really close to them are aware of their true identities. Covert manipulators will often exploit the targets of their schemes for extended periods of time, during which the targets may or may not be aware of the manipulation. They do this by confusing victims with their proverbial two faces, one of which is harsh while the other is compassionate and kind. They exploit cognitive dissonance to their advantage in order to achieve this.

The most effective strategy for avoiding people who are skilled at manipulating others is to be on the lookout for covert cues in their communication, such as changes in tone and body language, as well as an overemphasis on the positive aspects of their character.

The second kind of manipulation is more overt and often takes the form of physical contact. The manipulators often have some authority over the people they are trying to control, which makes it difficult to defeat them. In addition to this, unlike covert manipulators, they are not required to conceal their method. Idi Amin, Robert Pickton, and Russel Williams were brought up as examples of this kind of manipulation, and their respective instances were reviewed. In each instance, the manipulators did not attempt to conceal their goals; rather, they just carried out their plans in the manner that best suited them. Aside from the bully, the others benefited from significant social positions that shielded them from any adverse effects that may have been caused by the activities they took in the beginning. Overt manipulators are egotistical and unconcerned with the anguish they inflict on others, as seen by the acts they have taken in the past, which have shown this to be the case. In addition to this, they are cruel and will not think twice about inflicting all kinds of insults on the people they kill.

It is quite evident that a manipulator is never worried about the target, and this is true regardless of the form of manipulation being used. Because of this, the most effective method for defending oneself against them is to prevent manipulation as much as possible before it even begins, and to recognise it as soon as it occurs.   it.

Chapter Sixty-One

This a book has investigated a suppressed condition that is present in all individuals and that may drive people to prey on other people. There are a lot of individuals who are perfectly capable of controlling it, but there are also a few who have a tendency to act on their impulses to hurt other people or take advantage of them. The goal of dark psychology is to provide an explanation for this situation and how it manifests itself. The dark singularity, the dark factor, and the dark continuum are three essential characteristics of dark psychology that are addressed in the book. The black singularity is a region of the mind where inherently corrupt ideas may be found. The cravings to engage in harmful behavior that bring one closer to the dark singularity are known as dark factors. The dark singularity may be reached by following the dark continuum in its entirety. Humans go one step closer to the dark singularity each time they act on what are known as the dark factors, which are drives to do damage to other people.

Psychopaths and narcissists are labels that are usually used to those who have previously shown predatory conduct against other people. On the other hand, it is difficult to distinguish these folks from a typical person at a glance. This is due to the fact that they have a typical look and manner of talking, in addition to being very crafty and careful in their planning. On the other hand, they are secretly planning to take advantage of other people at some point in the future when the circumstances are favorable.

The contrast between dark psychology and traditional psychology has been highlighted by the fact that although the two are similar, dark psychology is not the same. The study of the human mind and behavior in its most basic form is known as normal psychology. It encompasses a number of subfields, the majority of which tend to concentrate on phenomena that are considered to be somewhat frequent in the culture, such as emotional illnesses, depression, and deviant patterns of thought and behavior. Dark psychology, on the other hand, places more of an emphasis on the suppressed state that leads people to behave as predators against one another. As a result of this, the field of dark psychology is restricted to the study of disorders in the human brain that lead people to prey on other people.

Both covert and overt manipulation, which are both prevalent in today's culture, are discussed in this book. Both forms of predation are a problem. Covert manipulation is a more delicate kind of manipulation in which the manipulators aim to establish influence over their targets by using disguised tactics. Covert manipulation is a sort of subtle manipulation. This kind of predatory behavior is typical in intimate relationships, and it often continues for extended periods of time before the victim realizes that they are being used in this way. Victimhood, gaslighting, time pressure, the silent treatment, guilt trips, and other covert manipulation tactics are some of the covert manipulation techniques. On the other hand, overt manipulation tactics are straightforward, aim for rapid success, and are most effective when used against complete strangers or those with connections that are at a distance from one another. Deception, corporal punishment, and the false assumption of blame are all examples of these strategies.

Getting individuals to do or agree to things that they would not normally want to do or agree to is one of the most significant challenges that dark psychology faces. It should go without saying that no one would knowingly choose to be the victim of predation. Therefore, manipulators need to be skilled in the art of persuasion in order to be successful against the people they are trying to control. The book delves into a number of tried-and-true methods of persuasion that may be used to other people in order to assert one's authority over them. Reciprocation, duty, concession, scarcity, commitment and consistency, like, social evidence, and framing are some examples of these types of social influences. The employment of these strategies might lead its targets to make rash choices, which works out to the benefit of the manipulators who use them.

The idea that words are potent and have the ability to change one's surroundings is one of the many encouraging and thought-provoking take-aways from this book. Words are the tool of choice for manipulators who want to take advantage of others. One may, however, become resistant to manipulation and even be able to influence others if they grasp the power of their own words and can communicate effectively with others. To put one's words to good use, one must first be familiar with and adhere to the fundamentals of sound communication in order to increase the likelihood that what they have to say will be heard. Listening, comprehending the viewpoint of the audience, validating the experiences of others, and having an awareness of oneself are all included in these concepts. After gaining an understanding of these fundamentals, one may exert influence on other people by interfering with the decisions they are making. Priming is a technique that often accomplishes this goal by implanting certain thoughts into the subconscious minds of other people. People may be influenced in a variety of ways, including those discussed in the book, including to be more honest, collaborative, and individualistic. Priming is an effective method for convincing individuals to make choices that have already been decided upon, and it is also a strategy that may be used either as a countermeasure or as a tactic for manipulating people.

The indicators that manipulators seek for in order to select the perfect victims are discussed in the book. Sadly, both nature and upbringing endow persons with some traits that may be utilized to abuse them in some way. The guilt conscience, the moral obligation to assist, the desire to avoid difficulty, and respect for authority are all qualities that fall under this category. These qualities characterize an individual's personality and are often used to classify individuals into categories. They are also useful for distinguishing people that are easily manipulated from other potential victims. The goal of manipulators is often to find some weakness signs in the personalities of their targets in order to identify those individuals who are likely to be vulnerable targets. The characteristics of innocence, honesty, materialism, elderliness, desire to please, poor self-reliance, pollyannaism, and lack of assertiveness are some of the indicators of vulnerability that are discussed in the book.

It has been shown via a number of case studies what a terrible impact it has when people prey on other humans. Overt manipulators may have far more severe repercussions, such as mass massacres, on the lives of their victims than covert manipulators do, which includes destroying relationships and making their victims' life unlivable forever. As a result, dark psychology sheds light on an essential characteristic of humans, namely that they are capable of becoming the cruellest creatures. The reality of the situation is that manipulation is something that can happen to anybody, that it becomes worse with time, and that it can be prevented.

Because it is shown in the book that everyone possesses the qualities that are targeted by both covert and overt manipulators, it is absolutely necessary to understand how to prevent oneself from being manipulated. This book provides an overview of a number of the strategies that renowned psychologists have suggested might be used by individuals in order to protect themselves against being exploited by other people. These strategies include taking your time to avoid being rushed, saying "no" emphatically and unequivocally to decisions that require it, being willing to compromise any choices made while being manipulated, tolerating any uncomfortable feelings that one may be exposed to as a result of being manipulated, calling out and disrupting the manipulation, and taking responsibility for any decisions made while being manipulated. When a manipulator discovers that the target is unwilling to cooperate or is too powerful to deceive, they will ultimately give up and stop trying to manipulate them. However, if a person is considered to be accommodating of any manipulation tactics, the people who are doing the manipulating will see that person as a vulnerable target and will continue to use exploitative techniques on them.

CPSIA information can be obtained
at www.ICGtesting.com
Printed in the USA
LVHW081742081022
730229LV00007B/97

9 781804 776483